EKLOGAI

Studies in Honour of Thomas Finan and Gerard Watson

edited by
Kieran McGroarty

Published by the Department of Ancient Classics, NUI Maynooth

Printed at the Cardinal Press, Convent Rd., Maynooth

ISBN 0-901519-34-0

The cover photograph is of a Christian tombstone from Aquileia (NE Italy), 5th century AD. The deceased is shown at the centre being baptized. As such the stone shows the coming together of the Classical and Christian traditions and so epitomises the academic endeavours of the honorands.

Photograph © Mark Humphries

CONTENTS

LIST OF CONTRIBUTORS

George Huxley is Honorary Professor of Greek at Trinity College, Dublin.

James McEvoy is Professor of Philosophy, Dean of the Faculty of Philosophy, NUI Maynooth and PU.

Kieran McGroarty is Lecturer in Classics at NUI Maynooth.

Maeve O'Brien is Lecturer in Classics at NUI Maynooth.

Thomas O'Loughlin is Senior Lecturer in the Department of Theology & Religious Studies at the University of Wales, Lampeter.

John O'Meara is Emeritus Professor of Latin at University College, Dublin.

Martin Pulbrook is a former lecturer in Classics at Maynooth; now employed in journalism.

Keith Sidwell is Professor of Latin and Greek at NUI Cork.

David Woods is College Lecturer in Ancient Classics at NUI Cork.

INTRODUCTION

Kieran McGroarty

The purpose of this Festschrift is to celebrate the scholarship of Professors Thomas Finan and the late Gerard Watson. It was conceived as a departmental Festschrift, with the addition of invited contributions, which would mark the retirement of two eminent scholars. Many of the contributors worked alongside the honorands, at one time or another, or had close scholarly contacts. The contributions therefore, carry not only new scholarly research, but genuine warmth and affection.

The title 'Eklogai' is quite appropriate to sum up the content of this book, given that the contributors work in so many different fields. Articles range from analysis of Aristotle's *Poetics* to the career of St. Patrick yet, even so, it is difficult to imagine any of the content would actually range or have ranged outside of the vast learning of the honorands.

I would like to thank, first and foremost, the contributors to this Festschrift. They responded to my missives with great speed and a clear desire to see the project completed and the honorands lauded. I hope that I have done justice to their professionalism and obvious enthusiasm. I want also to thank NUI Maynooth and the NUI Publications Scheme for generous contributions towards the printing costs. Thanks also to the Cardinal Press for their speedy production of the book. I am grateful to the following for their assistance: Patrick Devine, Monica Gale, David Scourfield and Richard Watson. Finally, I would like to thank all the staff of the department of Classics at Maynooth for their help and support, but in particular, I must mention Mark Humphries who might easily be credited as joint editor so much time and effort did he invest.

PROFESSOR THOMAS FINAN

Maeve O'Brien

I first met Professor Thomas Finan fifteen years ago. My Ph.D. was still a year or two in the future and he from the first was generous but never intrusive with his vast knowledge of the Classics.

Tom is a real humanist with a very dry wit. *Hic, pagani nos omnes,* was one of his first quips to me as I ventured on my lecturing career at Maynooth. His interests lie in the classics' Virgil, Homer and ancient Epic. Despite his quip, he is equally happy in Augustine studies. Greek and Roman art, ancient drama, and medieval Latin Lyric were just some of the areas he delighted in teaching. Many generations of students were privileged to be taught by him because he made Maynooth a place where *"all grew friendly for a little while"* (W.B. Yeats, *The dedication to a book of stories from the Irish novelists*). The Irish novelist George Moore is one of Tom's abiding interests. Though recently retired, Tom has published, and continues to publish, in the areas of Patristic Christology, on Thomas More, and intriguingly Ulysses and the Irish God. In 1998, he was active in attracting an international group of scholars of Thomas More to an important conference at Maynooth. The conference programme itself, both in content and style was a work of art.

A native of Sligo, Tom was ordained in 1956. A colleague of Tom's at that time, now retired, a distinguished member of the diplomatic corps, remembers well their long train journeys from the west 'with cardboard suitcases' Maynooth bound. Tom has soldiered, as he would put it, in Maynooth from his youth to his retirement in 1996. He was appointed Professor of Ancient Classics in October 1959, very early in a long career dedicated unselfishly to the promotion of the Classics, and especially study of the Latin language, in Maynooth and in Ireland. He is now making pleasant and scholarly use of his freer time taking many trips to Italy and especially to France. He follows in the steps of Thomas Hibernicus who made his mark as a classical scholar in France early in the fourteenth century. This worthy man's *Manipulus Florum* published at Piacenza in 1483, has the distinction of being the first printing of a book by an Irish person. We trust that the *nugae* in this *libellus* may divert our present day Thomas Hibernicus. In the words of another countryman, Patrick Kavanagh:

> *Tranquillity walks with me*
> *And no care.*
> *O, the quiet ecstasy*
> *Like a prayer.*
>
> *I find a star-lovely art*
> *In a dark sod.*
> *Joy that is timeless! O heart*
> *That knows God!*

We wish him many happy times, tranquillity, and no care.

THOMAS FINAN: BIBLIOGRAPHY

David Woods

1960 [1] 'Hellenistic Humanism in the Book of Wisdom', *Irish Theological Quarterly* 27, pp. 30-48.

1961 [2] 'Hellenism and Judeo-Christian History in Clement of Alexandria', *Irish Theological Quarterly* 28, pp. 83-114.
[3] 'Liturgical Arts', *The Furrow: Sacred Art Supplement* 4, pp. 41-2.

1962 [4] 'Irish Sacred Art', *The Furrow: Sacred Art Supplement* 5, pp. 1-6.

1963 [5] 'Thoughts on Sunday', *The Furrow* 14, pp. 702-08.
[6] 'Sacred Art and Architecture', *The Furrow: Sacred Art Supplement* 9, pp. 1-4.

1974 [7] 'What is Mortal Sin?', *The Furrow* 25, pp. 227-31.

1978 [8] 'Some More Comforts: More and the Consolatory Tradition', *Irish Theological Quarterly* 45, pp. 205-16.
[9] 'The Future of Maynooth: Ideals and Principles', *The Maynooth Review* 4.1, pp. 35-52.
[10] 'Catechesis Now and Then', *The Furrow* 29, pp. 28-37.

1979 [11] 'Total Tragedy and Homer's *Iliad*', *The Maynooth Review* 5.1, pp. 71-83.
[12] 'In Front of Our Future: The Pope at Maynooth', *The Furrow* 30, pp. 691-96.

1981 [13] 'Texts without Comment', *Irish Theological Quarterly* 48, pp.161-65.

1982 [14] 'Total Tragedy and the Epic of Gilgamesh', *The Maynooth Review* 7 (1982), pp. 3-16.
[15] 'Blood-dimmed Tide: Thoughts on the Apocalypse', *The Furrow* 33, pp. 659-66.

1985 [16] 'The Myth of the Innocent Sufferer: Some Greek Paradigms', *Proceedings of the Irish Biblical Association* 9, pp. 121-35.

1986 [17] 'Dante and the Religious Imagination' in J.P. Mackey (ed.), *Religious Imagination*, Edinburgh University Press, Edinburgh, pp. 65-85.
[18] 'The Poetic Imagination', *Irish Theological Quarterly* 52, pp. 66-80

1987 [19] 'St. Augustine', *The Furrow* 38, pp. 293-303.

1989 [20]'Hiberno-Latin Christian Literature', in J.P. Mackey (ed.), *An Introduction to Celtic Christianity*, T. & T. Clark, Edinburgh, pp. 64-100.

1990 [21] 'A Poet in Glass', *The Furrow* 41, pp. 147-55.

1991 [22] 'A Mystic in Milan: *reverberasti* revisited', in F.X. Martin and J.A. Richmond (edd.), *From Augustine to Eriugena: Essays on Neoplatonism and Christianity in Honour of John O'Meara*, CUA Press, Washington, D.C., pp. 77-91.

1992 [23] Joint-editor with V. Twomey of *The Relationship between Neoplatonism and Christianity: Proceedings of the First Patristic Conference at Maynooth 1990*, Four Courts Press, Dublin, to which he contributed 'Modes of Vision in St. Augustine: *De Genesi ad litteram* XII', pp. 141-54.
[24] 'Vision and Visionaries – What to Make of Them?', *The Furrow* 43, pp. 147-57.

1993 [25] Co-editor with P. Bastable *et alii* and contributor to *The Letters of Saint Patrick: A Study of their Theological Dimension*, by Daniel Conneely, An Sagart, Maynooth.

1995 [26] Joint-editor with V. Twomey of *Scriptural Interpretation in the Fathers: Proceedings of the Second Patristic Conference at Maynooth 1993*, Four Courts Press, Dublin, to which he contributed

'St. Augustine on the *mira profunditas* of Scripture: Texts and Contexts', pp. 163-99.

[27] Review-article on A. Dalzell and C.G. Nauert, *Erasmus: The Collected Works in English, Vol. 11: The Correspondence: Letters 1535-1657* in *Moreana* 122, pp. 71-97.

1996 [28] 'International Thomas More Conference 1998: Call for Papers', *Moreana* 127, pp. 5-36.

[29] 'Quelques possibilités pour des séances à sujets francais', *Moreana* 127, pp. 31-36.

[30] '*Non In Dialectica*? (M. Hoffmann, *Rhetoric and Theology: The Hermeneutic of Erasmus*)', *Moreana* 127, pp. 133-50.

1996/7[31] 'Ulysses and the Irish God', a review-article in *Irish Theological Quarterly* 62, pp. 38-48.

1997 [32] 'Homily at the Mass for the Opening of the Academic Year: 9 October 1996', *Maynooth University Record*, pp. 11-15.

[33] Review-article on Clarence H. Miller and Harry Vredeveld, *Collected Works of Erasmus, Volumes 85-86, Poems* in *Moreana* 34, no.130, pp. 85-99.

1998 [34] Joint-editor with V. Twomey of *Studies in Patristic Christology: Proceedings of the Third Patristic Conference at Maynooth 1996,* Four Courts Press, Dublin, to which he contributed 'The Desired of All Nations', pp. 1-22.

[35] 'International Thomas More Conference 1998: Programme', *Moreana* 133, pp. 5-28.

1999 [36] 'The Canonisation of Edith Stein', *Irish Theological Quarterly* 64, pp. 79-82.

[37] 'The Trinity in Early Irish Christian Writing' *Proceedings of the Fourth Patristic Conference at Maynooth*, forthcoming.

2000 [38] 'The influence of Lucian in the Writings of Sir Thomas More' *Proceedings of the Cambridge Conference of the International Association for Neo-Latin Studies*, forthcoming.

Thomas Finan is currently editing for publication papers developed from the 1998 International Thomas More Conference under the title *Thomas More and His Seasons: Humanism, Law, Theology*. He is also working on a paper for the forthcoming International Thomas More Conference to be held in France in 2001.

PROFESSOR GERARD WATSON

Kieran McGroarty

Professor Gerard Watson had become a major figure in St. Patrick's College, Maynooth, long before I came to know him. Ordained in 1959, he took up a teaching position, in the same year, in the Department of Greek and Latin at Maynooth. Concurrently, he enrolled for a PhD at the Queen's University, Belfast, which resulted in his first monograph, *The Stoic Theory of Knowledge*. He was then in a department of three, which included Professor William Meany and Professor Thomas Finan.

A man of keen intelligence and tremendous energy, he was to become a major force in the development of the College. He served on numerous committees including a period as secretary to the College Executive Council. He was one of a number of people behind a letter to Cardinal Conway, then Chairperson of the Trustees, which urged the opening up of the College to lay students. This was a landmark in the history of what is today NUI Maynooth. His efforts though were not confined to the sphere of university life. In 1978 he was elected to membership of the Royal Irish Academy and became Senior Vice-President for the year 1987-88. As one aware of the fact that nothing happens without the sacrifice of time and effort, he went on to serve as Secretary to the Academy from 1989 to 1993. While engaged in this activity, Gerard Watson had also by the mid-1970s become head of the Department of Greek and Latin at Maynooth. The department now consisted of four, a number that under his tutelage would increase to six with my own appointment in 1993.

I first met Gerard Watson in 1982, at the beginning of the second year of my undergraduate degree. My first encounter with him was in his role of teacher, and though we were to become great friends, it was to some extent as a teacher that he made his greatest impact on me. The ability to teach is a gift. It is a gift that he had in abundance. I remember with great clarity his lectures on Plato, St. Augustine, Tacitus and Alexander the Great. He had little need of the technical teaching aids available today; he sat, he talked and he captivated.

In 1993 I became his colleague. It was only then that I realised the weight of the administrative load that he had been carrying. In a department of six with over two hundred first year students it was a heavy burden. Any head of department will realise the extent of the work involved in catering for over three hundred and fifty students each year. It was a task that he made look easy. His door was always open and he always had time for students, which was reflected in the friendships he made and the sizeable correspondence that he maintained with past pupils.

This is all the more remarkable when you look at his publishing record which is being celebrated by this *Festschrift*. Apart from the five monographs, scholarly articles were published in prestigious encyclopaediae such as *ANRW* and journals such as the *Classical Quarterly*. Periodicals in this country were not neglected with many contributions being made to the *Irish Theological Quarterly* and the *Maynooth Review*. Through this work Gerard Watson gained an international reputation and established himself as a leading scholar in the areas of Greek philosophy and Patristics. It is a reputation that will endure.

Throughout his career, in spite of a heavy teaching load and substantial publication commitments, Gerard Watson also gave time to the promotion of the classical world in Ireland and abroad. For a number of years during part of his summer vacation, he taught Greek to beginners in classes organised by the Royal Irish Academy's National Committee for Greek and Latin Studies. This was never considered a chore but rather a labour of love.

Many people are good in one or another of the areas I have touched on above. It is very seldom that anyone excels in all of them, yet that has been his achievement. It has been my privilege to record it. It is with great sadness that I add the rider that Gerard Watson passed away during the preparation of this *Festschrift*. His absence is keenly felt.

GERARD WATSON: BIBLIOGRAPHY

Kieran McGroarty

1964 [1] 'Thoughts on Sunday', *The Furrow*, vol. 15, pp. 703-708.

1965 [2] 'Something Greater than the Iliad?' *Irish Ecclesiastical Record*, vol. civ, pp. 86-91.

1966 [3] *The Stoic Theory of Knowledge*, Belfast, Queen's University.
[4] 'The Early History of Natural Law', *Irish Theological Quarterly*, vol. xxxiii, pp. 65-74.

1969 [5] 'Greek Philosophy and Christian Ethics' in J.P. Mackey (ed.), *Morals, Law and Authority*, Dublin, Gill and Macmillan, pp. 39-57.

1970 [6] 'The Theology of Plato and Aristotle', *Irish Theological Quarterly*, vol. xxxvii, pp. 56-64.

1971 [7] 'The Natural Law and Stoicism' in A.A. Long (ed.), *Problems in Stoicism*, London, The Athlone Press, pp. 216-238.
[8] 'Aristotle's Concept of Matter', *Philosophical Studies*, vol. xx, pp. 175-184.

1973 [9] *Plato's Unwritten Teaching*, Dublin, Talbot Press.

1974 [10] 'Kafka: the Conversation under the Words', *Era*, vol. 1, pp. 35-44.

1975 [11] 'The Universal Language', *Maynooth Review*, vol. 1, no. 2, November, pp. 3-16.
[12] 'A Note on Lonegran and a Greek Conception of Science' in P. Corcoran (ed.), *Looking at Lonegran's Method*, Dublin, Talbot Press, pp. 55-58.

1979 [13] 'Greek Philosophy and Christian Theology' in P. Surlis (ed.), *Models of God*, New York.

1982 [14] 'St. Augustine's Theory of Language', *Maynooth Review*, vol. 6, no. 2, May, pp. 4-20.
[15] 'All his Works and Pomps', *Maynooth Review*, vol. 7, pp. 53-57.
[16] 'Φαντασία in Aristotle, *De Anima* 3.3', *Classical Quarterly*, 32, (i) pp. 100-113.
[17] 'Unfair to Proclus', *Phronesis*, vol. xxvii, no. 1, pp.101-106.

1983 [18] 'St. Augustine, the Platonists and the Resurrection of the Body: Augustine's Use of a Fragment of Porphyry', *Irish Theological Quarterly*, vol. 50, pp. 222-232.
[19] 'Crime and Punishment in Augustine and the Philosophical Tradition', *Maynooth Review*, vol. 8, May, pp. 32-42.

1984 [20] 'Ireland: Greek and Latin Philology in the Twentieth Century' in *La Filologia Greca e Latina nel secolo XX*, Rome, Atti del Congresso Internazionale, vol. II, pp. 983-1002.

1985 [21] 'Plato and the Story' in D.J. O'Meara (ed.), *Platonic Investigations*, Washington, Catholic University of America Press, pp. 35-52.
[22] 'The Problem of the Unchanging in Greek Philosophy' in *Neue Zeitschrift für Systematische Theologie und Religionsphilosophie*, 27 Band, Heft 1, pp. 57-70.
[23] 'I Doubt, Therefore I Am: St. Augustine and Scepticism', *Maynooth Review*, vol. 12, May, pp. 42-50.

1986 [24] 'Imagination and Religion in Classical Thought' in J.P. Mackey (ed.), *Religious Imagination*, Edinburgh: Edinburgh University Press, pp. 29-54.
[25] 'Imagination: The Greek Background', *Irish Theological Quarterly*, vol. 52, no. 1, pp. 54-65.

1987 [26] 'Gregory of Nyssa's Use of Philosophy in the *Life of Moses*', *Irish Theological Quarterly*, vol. 53, no. 2, pp. 100-112.
[27] 'Augustine, Jerome and Their Reaction to Jovinianus: A Response to Dr. Wilson', *Milltown Studies,* 19/20, pp. 111-115.

1988 [28] *Phantasia in Classical Thought,* Galway, Galway University Press.

[29] 'St. Augustine and the Inner Word: the Philosophical Background', *Irish Theological Quarterly*, vol. 54, no. 2, pp. 81-92.

[30] 'Discovering the Imagination: Platonists and Stoics on *Phantasia*' in J. Dillon and A.A. Long (edd.), *The Question of Eclecticism*, Berkeley, University of California Press, pp. 208-233.

1989 [31] 'Plato's *Gorgias* and Aristotle', *Maynooth Review*, vol. 14, December, pp. 51-66.

[32] 'Souls and Bodies in Origen's *Peri Archon*', *Irish Theological Quarterly*, vol. 55, no. 3, pp. 173-192.

1990 [33] *St. Augustine's Soliloquies and the Immortality of the Soul: Introduction, Translation and Commentary,* Warminster, Aris & Phillips.

1991 [34] 'Celsus and the Philosophical Opposition to Christianity', *Irish Theological Quarterly*, vol. 58, no. 3, pp. 165-179.

1994 [35] *Greek Philosophy and the Christian Notion of God*, Blackrock, Columba Press.

[36] 'The Concept of "Phantasia" from the Late Hellenistic Period to Early Neoplatonism' in W. Hasse and H. Temporini (edd.), *Aufsteig und Niedergang der Römischen Welt*, Berlin/New York, De Gruyter, Teil II: Principat, 36.7, pp. 4765-4810.

[37] 'Cogitatio' and 'Cognitio' in C. Mayer (ed.), *Augustinus-Lexikon*, Basel, Schwabe & Co., Vol. 1, Fasc. 7/8, pp. 1046-1064.

1995 [38]'Origen and the Literal Interpretation of Scripture' in T. Finan and V. Twomey (edd.), *Scriptural Interpretation in the Fathers*, Dublin, Four Courts Press, pp. 75-84.

THEOCRITUS ON LIZARDS IN WALLS

George Huxley

Recalling pleasant conversations during walks in the demesne at Maynooth, I thought that a note upon a topic in *Poem VII* of Theocritus would honour appropriately Father Finan and the late Father Watson.

As the companions walked from the town of Kos to the Haleis in the heat of the day, they were not yet half-way when they were joined by Lycidas the goatherd. Lycidas asked Simichidas why he was striding out in the noon "when even the lizard sleeps in the wall and the tomb-crested larks flit not about" (lines 21-23).

Here we are concerned with the habits of the lizards, not of the larks. ἁνίκα δὴ καὶ σαῦρος ἐν αἱμασιαῖσι καθεύδει (line 22) [ἐφ' αἱμ. ALU][1] can mean that the lizard is sleeping on or in the wall at noontide. One kind of lizard found in walls or upon them was called by Ionians κροκόδιλος (Herodotus 2.69.3). Concerning the lizard and the wall in Theocritus K.J. Dover remarked:

> Lizards in fact (as one would expect of cold-blooded creatures) grow livelier as the heat of the day increases, and they seek the hottest places. Theokritus's idea that they retire for a rest assimilates them unthinkingly to birds and mammals.[2]

One may venture to suggest that the quoted judgement is rather severe towards Theocritus, who had a keen eye for living things. Many lizards seek out, and benefit from, great heat, but some are nocturnal and less active in daytime. Geckoes are especially pertinent here. Geckones are a Suborder of *Lacertilia*. The pupil contracts into a vertical slit and the eyes are almost destitute of eyelids. Thus they can easily give the impression of being asleep. They can sometimes adapt to the colour of the rocks upon which they bask, in this resembling the chamaeleon. They are able to swallow insects whole, owing to the wide oesophagus, and their hunting at night is much helped by their power to climb smooth vertical surfaces and

---

[1] Gow, A.S.F., *Theocritus I* (Cambridge, 1950), p.57, app. crit.
[2] Dover, K.J., *Theocritus. Select Poems* (London, 1971), p.152.

even to run upside-down along ceilings. The agility is due to the delicate structure of their digits and toes.[3]

Theocritus, it seems, was well aware of the contrast between the energy of the gecko at night and its comparative lassitude during the day whether in or on walls. I well remember thinking of Theocritus when during our excavations at Kastri in Kythera in the early 'sixties we saw geckoes in the evening emerging from holes in the walls of the dig-house to catch moths. Speedily they ran up or backed down the walls, darting at their prey with wondrous deftness. Whether or not the creatures were asleep within or upon the Koan walls in the heat of the day, Lycidas may well have had geckoes in mind as they waited to hunt in the cool of the evening.

---

[3] On geckoes see *Encyclopedia Britannica*[11] (Cambridge, 1910), Vol. XI, p. 546-7; Vol. XVI (1911), p. 824. The adhesion is due to hairs, called setae, on their toes; each seta has hundreds of spatulae and may exploit intra-molecular, van der Waals, forces for its stickiness, according to Robert Full and his colleagues at the University of California, Berkeley: see *The Economist* Vol. 355, No. 1874 (June 10th 2000), p. 134.

FRIENDSHIP AND MUTUAL DECEPTION IN BOOK IV OF THE *CONFESSIONS* OF AUGUSTINE

James McEvoy

On a visit to the U.S.A. some years ago I found that my hosts had hung a handsome poster in the hallway of their home, with the following words of St Augustine about friendship printed and decorated on it.

> Different were the experiences which in their company more fully captivated my soul: to make conversation, to share a joke, to perform mutual acts of kindness, to read together well-written books, to share in trifling and in serious matters, to disagree though without animosity — just as a person debates with himself — and in the very rarity of disagreement to find the salt of normal harmony, to teach each other something or to learn from one another, to long with impatience for those absent, to welcome them with gladness on their arrival. These and other signs come from the heart of those who love and are loved, and are expressed through the mouth, through the tongue, through the eyes, and a thousand gestures of delight, acting as fuel to set our minds on fire, and out of many to forge unity.[1]

The intention of my friends was, of course, the admirable one of creating an ambience of hospitable friendship in their home. However, my reaction disconcerted them, when I suggested that this passage should not be taken at face value but should be understood ironically, as giving expression to experiences and thoughts which the writer of the *Confessions* located far back in his own past, but to which he no longer subscribed in a straightforward way.

I   The 'Carthage Passage' in Recent Writings

It is true that, when taken out of context, this description of youthful friends makes an effect of simple charm. It recounts in vivid terms the attitudes and activities that fused their minds and hearts into unity. It has

---

[1] Adapted from Henry Chadwick, *St Augustine: Confessions* (Oxford, 1991), pp. 60-61.

even been described by a redoubtable authority as "a paean to friendship."[2] Some recent writers have come to the conclusion that this passage, together with its context, locates the youthful Augustine firmly within a fully classical conception of friendship, the key to which was provided for Augustine by Cicero, above all other Latin writers.[3] The distance between the author of the *Confessions* and his youthful self ('the artist as a young man', as one might say) is generally agreed to be attributable to that development which, initiated by his re-conversion and baptism, was to lead Augustine to formulate aspects of a Christian theory of love and friendship, in which he included elements of the classical outlook. Carolinne White, for instance, writes as follows:

> It is true that he became dissatisfied with a fundamentally humanistic form of friendship, adapting his view of the subject after his conversion in accordance with his new ideals and with a view of love derived from what St Paul and St John had said on the subject, as well as from the teachings and example of the incarnate Christ.[4]

White develops a balanced, dialectical point of view concerning both the discontinuities and the element of continuity that can be disclosed by the careful comparison of Augustine's earlier and later views about friendship. Referring to the passage which particularly occupies our attention in the present essay she has this to say:

> Augustine's experiences did provide some kind of model for the later forms of communal life which he organised. At Carthage, where he fled to try and forget his lost friend, he shared his life with a group of friends whose common interests (based on a commitment to Manichaeism) and mutual love offered him comfort. He describes vividly the attraction of these relationships at *Conf.* IV.viii.13; he may have come to regard

---

[2] James J. O'Donnell, *Augustine. Confessions, Vol. II, Commentary on Books 1-7* (Oxford, 1992), p. 217. This thorough study of the language, sources and thought of the *Confessions* is an indispensable aid to the serious study of the work.
[3] In the art. 'Amicitia' in the *Augustinus Lexikon* of Würzburg, Ilsetraut Hadot maintains that Seneca exercised a marked influence on Augustine's ideas about friendship; I find no evidence in support of this view.
[4] Carolinne White, *Christian Friendship in the Fourth Century* (Cambridge, 1992), p. 189.

them as wrong, but it is also clear that he looked back on them with nostalgia (pp. 211-212).

With these views, and with the broadly similar ones expressed by Tarcisius J. Van Bavel, O.S.A., regarding Augustine's references to Cicero, I find myself in general agreement.[5] It could even be said that at this stage some lines of interpretation of the passage that concerns us have been placed beyond dispute, so much common ground is there among recent writers. However, I should like to put forward the notion that the description of friendship set down by Augustine with reference to his Carthage period has a subversively ironical meaning, a meaning fully intended by its author but one which has practically escaped attention. The ironic distance which Augustine placed between his outlook as autobiographer (in A.D. 396-397) and his Carthage experience extends (so I shall argue) both to the classical conception of friendship and to the Manichaean setting in which the former was lived by the group to which he was attached. His irony can thus be understood for what it was in this application: a literary marker indicating the fall of his youthful self into a state of untruth, a lived myth which parodied that Truth which was in due course to win Augustine, against himself, for Itself.

The re-examination of the passage and of its context serves as an opportunity to review the invocation of the classical motifs concerning *amicitia* to which the passage makes allusion, and to evaluate the nature of their employment; for they are much more than simply decorative motifs. This inquiry offers a suitable occasion for honouring two Maynooth classicists, each of whom dedicated a portion of his research to the greatest of the African Catholic bishops.

---

[5] Tarsicius J. Van Bavel, 'The Influence of Cicero's Ideal of Friendship on Augustine', in *Augustiniana Traiectina*, eds. J. den Boeft and J. van Oort (Paris, 1987), pp. 59-72. The footnotes of this valuable article refer to the principal studies of *amicitia* in the thought of Augustine. Further bibliography can be located in White's book (referred to in n. 4), as well as in the footnotes of the following article: James McEvoy, '*Anima Una et Cor Unum*: Friendship and Spiritual Unity in Augustine', in *Recherches de Théologie ancienne et médiévale* 53 (1986), pp. 40-92. Among the more notable recent contributions to the study of friendship and charity in Augustine the following should be counted: Eoin Cassidy, 'The Recovery of the Classical Ideal of Friendship in Augustine's Portrayal of *Caritas*', in *The Relationship between Neoplatonism and Christianity*, eds. T. Finan and V. Twomey (Dublin, 1992), pp. 127-140; Luigi Pizzolato, *L'idea di amicizia nel mondo antico classico e cristiano,* Einaudi Paperbacks, Filosofia 238 (Milan, 1993), pp. 296-318.

II   The Setting of the Passage

At *Conf.* IV.vi.7 St Augustine narrates the formation of an early, deep friendship which he formed with a man of the same age (19-20), shortly after returning from his studies at Carthage to the village of Thagaste where they had gone to school and grown up together. Augustine turned him away from the Catholic faith, of which the young man had only an immature consciousness, and brought him into the company, and the faith, of the Manichees. Their friendship was sundered by the sudden death of this unnamed friend, who succumbed to a fever. He died at home. His family had him baptized while he lay ill and unconscious, for such was the custom among the Christians of North Africa.

The narrative account of this early friendship, together with the sequel (Augustine's expression of grief, his reflection on the power of tears, his idea of friendship) has (justly, it must be said) merited considerable attention during the past two decades. No doubt this is due to the contemporary rise in interest concerning bereavement and grieving, as well as regarding friendship and the historical forms it has taken. There can be no question of undertaking its fuller analysis in the present context.[6] Our aim is the more modest one of situating the passage we have chosen to analyse, within the context that opens with the narrative and extends to Augustine's evocation of intense grief at this early loss.

It may be noted at this point that it is Augustine's habit in the *Confessions* (and it is an aspect of his genius as revealed there) to link his reflections firmly to precise incidents occurring in his own life or in the lives of others close to him, that is to say, to moments of actual experience carefully situated in place and time. It is not of Friendship that Augustine writes, but rather of his friendship with this or that contemporary of his; it is not a treatise on bereavement and grief that he pens, instead it is the record of his own tears and terrors in the wake of the death of this particular friend. It is the conjoint form of loving and even (one might say) unremitting attention to the particular, together with his unerring ability to show the universal human quality as that was mirrored in his own personal experience, that sets Augustine's *Confessions* quite apart from other ancient writings

---

[6] See my art., referred to in n. 5, for an analysis of Augustine's expression of grief (pp. 69-72). The present study should be regarded as a footnote to the former one (1986).

making a significant use of the first person, such as the *Meditations* of Marcus Aurelius. This noble Roman Stoic had his gaze fixed inflexibly upon the unvarying ideal of human life, and he constantly invited both himself and his reader to 'test for yourself your capacity for the life of a good man'. The emperor's reflections were not only general, they were by nature and intention nothing less than universal, which is to say that he adverted to his own particular existence only in order to give expression to the constant regret that he could not more truly incarnate the perfect order of the universe in his life, actions and relationships.

III   Allusions to Classical Friendship and their Function

Through his choice of vocabulary, including words and phrases with a long history of Latin usage to characterise friends and friendship, Augustine related the reflective movements of his own thought to the classical tradition, and in a very special way to the *Laelius* of Cicero. Each of these linguistic and literary links deserves a moment's attention.

Orestes and Pylades

It is from *De Amicitia* 7:24 that Augustine borrowed the first of his allusions to Cicero's philosophy of friendship.[7] This pair of friends had acquired legendary status by Cicero's time, and indeed long before then. The unity of mind and purpose of the two lent them a powerful symbolic value, in view of the determination of each not to allow the other to die. The function of this paradigm in the *Confessions* seems to be to bring to forceful expression the abyss that yawns between a quasi-mythical, timeless symbol of friendship, on the one hand, and Augustine's existential suffering, on the other. "Traditur, si non fingitur", he remarked of the story alluded to by Cicero, thereby placing the literary reference on the level of *fabula*, i.e. a story handed down but without authentication, and hence difficult to situate with regard to historical reality.[8] The hard reality of his own experience, however, stubbornly refused to be conformed to the story, for he found himself caught up in a tension of equally violent and equally opposite emotional forces, neither of which bore any resemblance to the legend of Orestes and Pylades: he experienced *taedium vitae* on the one

---

[7] Cicero also mentions the pair in *De Finibus* 5.22.63. It was thence that St Ambrose derived his reference to these legendary friends, *De Officiis* 1.41.216.

[8] O'Donnell (in the work referred to in n. 2) comments aptly: "...the *exemplum* is just the sort of mythic context in which A. would have attempted to understand his own grief at the time."

hand (he was 'utterly weary of life') and on the other, *moriendi metus* ('fear of dying').

Is there a nuance of difference between Augustine's reaction to the Orestes and Pylades story and that of Cicero? Both writers appear to agree that these legendary friends displayed unity of determination and will. For Cicero, each of them showed himself willing to die in order to keep his *alter ipse* alive. Augustine changes the emphasis: neither friend wished to *live* without the other. This perhaps resonates with Augustine's feeling at the time of his youthful grief, or at least with an aspect of it.

ille alter eram
Cicero's Greek culture stood him in good stead when he came to write on friendship, for he had read (probably) the *Lysis* of Plato, one of Aristotle's accounts of *philia,* and the three books of Theophrastus on the same subject, which have survived in only a few fragmentary quotations by later writers.[9] Aristotle deliberately employed a number of proverbs and quasi-proverbial sayings (sixteen in all) concerning friendship, since he supposed that these incorporated the remains of an ancient, and otherwise lost, wisdom. In interpreting them, he endeavoured to raise them up to the philosophical level of his own thought.[10] The proverbial saying 'Another Hercules, another dear self' was understood by Aristotle to yield an answer to the question: can one ever love another as one loves oneself? Aristotle maintained that only by according to another person the same kind of love as that with which one treats oneself, may one come to regard that other, chosen friend as 'another self' (ἄλλος αὐτός). Cicero reproduced this thought with accuracy, referring to the friend as "tamquam alter idem".[11]

It is extremely unlikely that Augustine was aware of the Aristotelian origin of the *alter ipse* thought. He introduced it in the context of his love for the friend who died. He referred to himself as the 'other' of his friend ('quia

---

[9] The fragments have been gathered by W.W. Fortenbaugh *et al., Theophrastus of Eresus. Sources for his Life, Writings, Thought and Influence*, part 2, Philosophia Antiqua, 54, 2 (Leiden, 1992), nos. 532-546: Friendship (pp. 360-371). The possibility that Cicero was acquainted with the *Memorabilia* of Xenophon cannot be ruled out.
[10] J. McEvoy, 'Aristotelian Friendship in the Light of Greek Proverbial Wisdom', in *Aristotelica Secunda. Mélanges offerts à Christian Rutten,* eds. A. Motte and J. Denooz (Liège, 1996), pp. 167-179.
[11] *Laelius* 80; cf 22: 'sic loqui ut tecum'.

ille alter eram'), thus reversing the self-referring nature of the thought in a way that I have not seen paralleled in any ancient writing. Furthermore, he drew it out in the direction of another image, the 'half of the soul', in a way that gave the 'alter ipse' an unusual twist: in doing so he made an intimate link between two motifs that derived from quite different origins, the first coming from Aristotle, the second deriving from Plato's *Symposium*.[12]

dimidium animae

The 'someone' to whom Augustine referred as saying about his friend, 'the half of my soul', was not Cicero (who did not employ the Platonic metaphor), but Horace.[13] The philosophical origin of the saying is to be sought in the *Symposium*, in the speech of 'Aristophanes' (i.e. one of Plato's masks), which purports to recount by way of a myth the origin of sexual desire.[14] It goes like this: the original androgynous creation proved to be too self-reliant and godlike; Zeus determined to punish their hybris by cleaving each one into halves; for ever afterwards (and even now), each half becomes conscious of its incompleteness through the experience of sexual desire, in which the longing to be whole, once again, rises to the surface. St Augustine gives no sign of being aware of the philosophical origin of the metaphor he employs. The sense he gives it makes no reference to sexuality, but instead intends unity of soul, in the words which follow:

sensi animam meam et animam illius unam fuisse animam in duobus corporibus

---

[12] St Thomas Aquinas, in reference to this passage (and clearly under its influence), considered that 'alter ipse' and 'dimidium animae' both signified the intimate union which comes about between and among friends. However, he was not able to disentangle their different literary and philosophical origins, since his age had no access to the *Symposium*. *(Summa Theologiae* IaIIae, qu. 28, art 1, *in corpore*). See J. McEvoy, 'The Other as Oneself: Friendship and Love in the Thought of Thomas Aquinas', in *Maynooth University Record* 1 (1996) pp. 27-48; p. 41.

[13] Horace, *Carm.* 1.3.5-8:
> navis, quae tibi creditum
> debes Vergilium, finibus Atticis
> reddas incolumem precor,
> et serves animae dimidium meae.

[14] Plato, *Symp.* 189c-193d; cf. 205d. The notion of primordial hermaphrodites goes back to Empedocles, fr. 446.

Aristotle informs us that the saying 'friends are one soul' was proverbial. The actual phrase, 'one soul in two bodies', goes back to Diogenes Laertius, who in his Life of Aristotle attributed it to the philosopher, as being the latter's definition of friendship.[15] We can safely rule out the possibility that Augustine had it from that source, for his knowledge of Greek was, by his own admission, very limited. The saying does not occur in Cicero. Ovid is Augustine's likeliest source for it. Writing on Orestes and Pylades (*Tristia* 4.4.72) the poet concluded, "qui duo corporibus, mentibus unus erant."[16] There is evidence to suggest that by the fourth century A.D. the saying was current in both Greek and Latin languages. Writing of his friendship with St Basil, Gregory of Nazianzen said, "We had all things in common, and a single soul, as it were, bound together our two distinct bodies."[17] Writing some years after the *Confessions*, St John Cassian could speak of himself and Germanus as being "one mind and soul in two bodies."[18] The influence of Augustine is tangible in the dialogue of St Aelred of Rievaulx on friendship. He refers there to the spiritual unity of

---

[15] Diogenes Laertius, *Lives of Eminent Philosophers,* trs. R.D. Hicks (Loeb ed.), vol. I. Bk 5, 'Aristotle', c. 20 (p. 462).

[16] Ovid, *Tristia* 4.4.72.

[17] Gregory of Nazianzen, *De Vita Sua, P.G.* 37, col. 225ff; cf the funeral oration for Basil, *Or.* 43.20 (*P.G.* 36). A clear echo of this is to be heard in the commentary by Michael of Ephesus (12th cent.) on *Nicomachean Ethics* Bk IX, in the translation of Robert Grosseteste: 'Omnes homines, quando volumus ostendere quoniam hunc aliquem valde amamus, aimus quoniam una anima et ego et ipse sumus, quemadmodum et magnus in theologia dixit Gregorius in magni Basilii epitaphio: "Una anima in duobus corporibus." See *The Greek Commentaries on the 'Nicomachean Ethics' of Aristotle in the Latin Translation of Robert Grosseteste,* vol. III, ed. H. Paul F. Mercken, *Corpus Latinum Commentariorum in Aristotelem Graecorum,* VI, 3 (Leuven, 1991), pp. 229-30. Grosseteste employs a variant on the ancient saying in his own gloss on *Nicomachean Ethics* VIII: "Possunt etiam fratres dici *idem* ad invicem propter naturalem fraternum amorem, facientem eos 'cor unum et animam unam', *in* corporibus *divisis*." (The italicized words come from Grosseteste's version of Aristotle). See J. McEvoy, 'Grosseteste's Reflections on Aristotelian Friendship: A "New" Commentary on *Nicomachean Ethics* VIII. 8-14', in McEvoy J., ed., *Robert Grosseteste. New Perspectives on his Thought and Scholarship,* Instrumenta Patristica XXVII (Steenbrugge, in Abbatia Sti Petri/Kluwer Academic Publishers, 1994), pp. 149-168.

[18] John Cassian, *Conlatio* I.1., speaks of himself and Germanus in the following terms: "...ut cuncti ad significandum sodalitatis ac propositi nostri parilitatem pronuntiarent unam mentem atque animam duobus inesse corporibus."

friends in Christ as producing such holy delight that "there seems to be but one soul in different bodies."[19]

By this saying Augustine intended unity. In his eyes love creates, or tends to create, unity; and of course friendship is a form of love.

amantes et redamantes

Cicero appears to lay claim to the paternity of the word 'redamare'.[20] Augustine employs the linked words *amare/redamare* again in the immediate sequel to the Carthage passage.[21] On the second occasion he relates the mutual or reciprocal character of friendship to disinterestedness, that ethical apogée of the classical philosophy of friendship which Cicero opposed again and again to *utilitas*, where an interest of some kind is involved.[22]

ex pluribus unum

These words echo a phrase of Cicero, who maintained that the whole nature of friendship is to make "as it were one soul of many."[23] The 'unus animus' of Cicero could not fail to attract the attention of Augustine, especially so in the wake of the latter's rediscovery of the New Testament passage in which the earliest adherents of the new faith were referred to as being "one in heart *and soul*" (AA 4:32). This passage was to leave a profound mark upon Augustine's ecclesiology.

---

[19] *Aelredi Rievallensis Opera Omnia* (Corpus Christianorum Continuatio Mediaeualis 1), Turnhout 1971, *De Spirituali Amicitia* II.27: "illum sacratissimum amantibus inspirans affectum, ut uideatur illis quasi unam animam in diuersis esse corporibus." This saying is subtly implied in the same author's *Speculum Caritatis* I.34.112: "mirabar animam illam quae cum mea una erat, sine mea corporis exui posse compedibus."

[20] *Laelius* 49: "...eo qui uel amare uel, ut ita dicam, redamare possit, non admodum delectari?" *Redamare* translates *antifilein* (Plato, *Lysis,* 212 c-d).

[21] "Hoc est, quod diligitur in amicis et sic diligitur, ut rea sibi sit humana conscientia, si non amauerit redamantem aut si amantem non redamauerit, nihil quaerens ex eius corpore praeter indicia beniuolentiae." *Conf.* IV. ix. 14.

[22] "Nam si utilitas amicitias conglutinaret, eadem commutata dissolueret." *Laelius* 32.

[23] *Laelius* 92: "Nam cum amicitiae uis sit in eo, ut unus quasi animus fiat ex pluribus..." Cf *De Officiis* I.17.56, where virtuous friends are said to incarnate the ideal of Pythagoras, that many should become one ("ut unus fiat ex pluribus").

humaniter

Augustine reproached himself for his former 'madness', in not knowing how to love men in a human way ('diligere humaniter').[24] Now Ciceronian *humanitas* meant, in the context of friendship and love, experiencing the same joys and the same sorrows as one's friend, in an empathy which expressed in terms of feeling those very qualities of equality, similarity and unity that are the foundation of friendship itself.[25] *Humanitas* was, in short, the opposite of *severitas*, which was the object of the reproach of unfeelingness repeatedly made by Cicero to the early Stoa. Speaking of friendship, St Augustine resorts to an older classical meaning, expressed by the adverb 'humaniter' ('loving humans humanly'), by which was meant loving them 'not as though they were never to die', but rather as fellow mortals. Augustine had loved the friend he lost in a way that he himself later judged to be immoderate (*inmoderate*), that is to say, lacking in the measure that alone is proper to human existence: "ille quem quasi non moriturum dilexeram, mortuus erat."[26]

IV   Cicero's Definition of Friendship and the 'Carthage Passage'

Conf. IV.viii.13 locates Augustine at Carthage in the immediate wake of the death of his friend; for it was to there that he fled, in flight from his unhappy self. He made friends among the Manichees there. The description of their friendship (the passage which appeared in translation into English at the beginning of this essay) runs as follows:

> alia erant, quae in eis amplius capiebant animum, conloqui et
> conridere et uicissim beniuole obsequi, simul legere libros
> dulciloquos, simul nugari et simul honestari, dissentire interdum
> sine odio tamquam ipse homo secum atque ipsa rarissima
> dissensione condire consensiones plurimas, docere aliquid
> inuicem aut discere ab inuicem, desiderare absentes cum
> molestia, suscipere uenientes cum laetitia: his atque huius modi

---

[24] "O dementiam nescientem diligere homines humaniter! O stultum hominem inmoderate humana patientem! quod ego tunc eram." *Conf.* IV.viii.12.

[25] See, for instance, *Laelius* 8 and 50. The term appears to me to sustain much of the weight of Cicero's criticism of the rigidity (as he saw it) of the primitive Stoa regarding the feelings, the empathy and the intimacy that belong essentially to friendship.

[26] On friendship in relation to mortality in the *Confessions* see J. McEvoy, 'Liberty, Finitude and Transcendence. An Augustinian Hypothesis', in *At the Heart of the Real. Philosophical Essays in Honour of the Most Rev. Desmond Connell, Archbishop of Dublin,* ed. Fran O'Rourke (Dublin, 1992), pp. 373-380.

signis a corde amantium et redamatium procedentibus per os, per linguam, per oculos et mille motus gratissimos quasi fomitibus conflare animos et ex pluribus unum facere.

As we have already remarked, it is currently common ground among interpreters to regard the depiction of friendship offered here as incorporating values and behaviour corresponding to the classical ideal, as that was successfully epitomised by Cicero. Attention shall however be paid to what is missing, as well as to what is actually said. Both become evident once the comparison is made with the celebrated definition of friendship in terms of "agreement in all things divine and human, with good will and affection."[27] This definition can be placed like a stencil over the 'Carthage passage', to the following effect.

Consensio, that agreement which reflects the unity of friends, and which is of both the mind and the will, made up the foundation of the group's unity and was the norm (*consensiones plurimas*) of its members' relationship. Disagreements were rare; indeed, Augustine likens them to the differences one can sometimes have with oneself, in order thereby to indicate the high degree of unity that normally prevailed. Mutual good will, which the Greek and Latin thinkers who wrote on the topic of *philia/amicitia* all agreed in placing at the core of friendship, finds a clear reflection in the words *uicissim beneuole obsequi*: literally, to do each other those services that flow from good will.

A significant term in Cicero's definition, but on the other hand one which does not appear in the 'Carthage passage' is *caritas*. (Cicero employed this word consistently, to express the fondness and affection that belong essentially to friendship). Mutual love those Manichees certainly had. It finds expression (as we have seen) in the Ciceronian terms *amare et*

---

[27] "Est enim amicitia nihil aliud nisi omnium divinarum humanarumque rerum cum beneuolentia et caritate consensio." *Laelius* 20. Augustine refers to this definition in *Contra Academicos* 3,6,13, and several times in *Ep.* 258, 1-4. For a translation of most of this letter and some commentary, see my article, referred to in n. 5 (pp. 76-79. Père Maurice Testard has noted that when quoting the Ciceronian definition Augustine consistently reversed the order of the words 'divinarum et humanarum'. In this way the static outlook of the pagan, in which the *res divinae* have precedence in virtue of their greater dignity, is rendered theocentric, in accordance with the ascent-model of Augustine's thought; see M. Testard, *S. Augustin et Cicéron. I. Cicéron dans la formation et dans l'oeuvre de S. Augustin* (Paris, 1958), p. 270.

redamare, and equally in 'unity of spirit' (*spiritus, ex pluribus unum*). However, one will search in vain for the word '*caritas*'. Now, this omission simply cannot be innocent on Augustine's part. The interpreter is entitled, I think, to conclude from its absence that the author of the *Confessions* deliberately refused to employ the word *caritas* in relation to his Manichaean experiences of love and friendship, precisely because of all that the term had come to mean to him subsequent to his re-conversion to the Catholic Church. Augustinian *caritas* was the translation of the New Testament term ἀγαπή. It expressed the love of Christ and the very depths of God. It was certainly not to be used in a way that might confuse the reader of the conversion story, nor to be employed in any context that might give even the appearance of mitigating Augustine's retrospective denunciation of the untruth of the existence which he and his friends had led at Carthage.[28] That life was based, he reminds the reader, upon "an enormous fiction, a prolonged lie, by whose adulterous caressing my soul, with its itching ears [2 Tim 4:3-4] was corrupted." (My translation).

The depiction of friendship is placed in a setting that is dark and unpromising – but it brings some relief with it. The initial words of the 'Carthage passage' are indicative of a contrast with the preceding phrase, or at least are capable of being read in that light: *Alia* erant quae... ('Different [from the foregoing fiction and corrupting lie] were the experiences which in their company more fully captivated my soul'). Augustine was in time to repudiate 'the lie' of the Manichees, but he had no wish to annul in his memory the experience of friendship in their company. In the lines following the depiction he repeats that friendship of its essence calls for the reciprocal expression of love and goodwill, and that it produces such affective unity that the death of any one of our friends makes a living death of our own life. The author of the *Confessions* did not deny the human value of the friendship he experienced at as a youth at Carthage, instead he showed it in its incompleteness and its inherent longing for a truth which it itself could not as yet express, but only dumbly desire, as its own inner finality and perfect realisation.

---

[28] Speaking of the Manichaean circle, and referring to his friends within it, Augustine says "cum quibus amabam quod pro te amabam, et hoc erat ingens fabula et longum mendacium, cuius adulterina confricatione corrumpebatur mens nostra pruriens in auribus." (Cf. II Tm 4:3-4).

The friendship which Augustine knew at Carthage was shared by the members of a coterie, in other words it was retained within the strict limits of a circle of initiates. It is known that the exercise of hospitality was forbidden to the *auditores* of Manicheanism, who were indeed permitted to give to the poor, but only in money, never food.[29] Is it surprising that, looking back to that enclosed experience, Augustine should refuse to apply the sacred term *caritas* to the friendship which bound together the members of that self-selecting group? Did he consider that a friendship to which hospitable outreach to the neighbour as such was forbidden was not worthy to be described in terms that are alone appropriate to that love which is meant to reach out to all, without exclusion? It was not for nothing that the author of the *Regula Augustini* (which was composed prior to the *Confessions*) made hospitality the foremost obligation of the monk. In this particular just as in others (for instance, the regular partaking of meat and wine at table), the community founded by the Bishop of Hippo presented a profile quite opposed, and of course consciously opposed, to the founder's own former Manichaean practice.

The paragraph which immediately follows upon the 'Carthage passage' draws an explicit lesson for the reader. Augustine refers back to that experience of unity which is at the depth of mutual love, and which is expressed in outward signs of good will. When death comes to sunder deep unity it leaves the survivors in 'a living death'. The lesson is placed squarely before the reader. It sets the tone for the subsequent reflections of Augustine:

> Happy is the person who loves you [Tobit 13:18] and his friend
> in you, and his enemy because of you [cf. Matt 5:44].[30]

The beatitude ('*beatus qui*') is drawn from the Book of Tobit. In the Old and New Testaments this formulaic utterance conveys the meaning that happiness is conferred by God himself on "those who hear his word and keep it" (Lk 11:28), welcoming as they do the promise it brings with it. By

---

[29] John O'Meara summarizes the practices of the Manichees in *The Young Augustine* (London, 1954,1980), ch. iv.

[30] "beatus qui amat te et amicum in te et inimicum propter te. solus enim nullum carum amittit, cui omnes in illo cari sunt, qui non amittitur." *Conf.* IV.ix.14. Cf. *De Doctrina Christiana* 1, XXII 20-21 for a very central statement concerning *amor ordinatus*, or loving all 'in God.'

juxtaposing the two biblical allusions Augustine evoked the entire law of what he famously called *amor ordinatus*, which is to say, that love which comes to the believer from God, and which enfolds enemies as well as friends — and does so, moreover, in death as much as in life. The very truth of love is to be found in the Truth which is God himself. In God, no one who is dear to us is lost: that is the claim, and at the same time the challenge to faith and trust, which Augustine advances here, and places before both himself and his reader.

The foregoing affirmation, made in faith, takes up again the pronouncement concerning *vera amicitia,* which Augustine included in the narrative of his friendship with the man who died young (*Conf.* IV.iv.7), contrasting that friendship with the Christian experience which, he states, was at that moment unknown to them both:

> Neither in those earlier days, nor indeed in the later time of which I now speak, was he a friend in the truest meaning of friendship; for there is no true friendship unless You weld it between souls that cleave together through that "charity which is shed in our hearts by the Holy Ghost who is given to us" [Rm 5:5].[31]

It is worth noting here that Romans 5:5 frequently served Augustine as an epitome of the New Law, which is not a re-statement of the Ten Commandments but rather the gift which the Spirit of Pentecost pours into the hearts of believers.[32]

V   Friendship and the Other Themes of *Confessions* Book IV

The interpretation we have offered here of the 'Carthage passage' on friendship deserves to be tested. How does it sit with the themes that predominate in the fourth book of the *Confessions*? It will be argued in what follows that this book possesses a thematic unity, of which the account of friendship forms a strand that is consistent with the whole.

---

[31] "sed nondum erat sic amicus, quamquam ne tunc quidem sic, uti est uera amicitia, quia non est uera, nisi cum eam tu agglutinas inter haerentes sibi caritate diffusa in cordibus nostris per spiritum sanctum, qui datus est nobis."

[32] A fine example of this interpretation, an example chosen out of many possible candidates, is St Augustine's *Sermo* 34 (*CCL* 41, pp. 424-426).

The preface to the fourth book enunciates its themes in the clearest of terms. The opening lines indicate the descent that took place, as the youthful Augustine repeated in his own way the fall of Adam:

> During this same period of nine years, from my nineteenth to my twenty-eighth year, our life was one of being seduced and seducing, being deceived and deceiving, in a variety of desires.[33]

Ambition in professional life and enrolment in a false religion serve as headings for this chapter of the *Confessions*. However, the detailed story includes the taking of a woman as a partner, and becoming entrapped in the delusion of astrology. In introducing this period of his life Augustine speaks of "myself and my friends who had been *deceived through me and with me*" — referring to friends made within the circle of the Manichees.[34] When he comes to recount his friendship with the unnamed young man of Thagaste he stresses the religious bond between them, alluding to his own successful efforts to bring his friend into the Manichaean fold:

> I had turned him away from the true faith, to which, being only young, he had no strong or profound allegiance, towards those superstitious and pernicious mythologies (*fabellas*) which were the reason for my mother's tears over me.

Augustine's grief for his dead friend sent him off on a vain search for religious consolation - vain, because an 'empty phantasm' cannot be made to sustain the weight of real feeling. It is into the narrative account of that friendship and that death, which is followed by the description of his own grief, that the depiction of the friendships which Augustine made at Carthage is slipped. Given the context, it is not to be expected that he would paint those friendships in an altogether favourable light. He formed them, he tells us, while in flight from himself and in dread of his own mortality. Looking back upon that period of his life he was struck by his own immaturity.[35] What he described was the experience of a coterie which was closed off in great measure from the outside world, a garden full

---

[33] The allusion to II Tim 3:13 is clear.

[34] *Conf.* IV.i.1.

[35] This was the aspect of the depiction which was to impress St Aelred of Rievaulx most forcibly; see 'Postscript.'

of beautiful souls whose friendship was aesthetic and sentimental rather than truly spiritual.

The remainder of book IV offers support for the interpretation of the 'Carthage passage' which has been advanced here. Augustine seeks through the therapy of 'confession' (which is at once praise of God and acknowledgement of past failure and present vulnerability), to deepen his own apprehension of the fundamental truth that the enjoyment of mutable things is bound to become bitter to the taste unless they are loved 'in God, who is never lost.' Mortal loves, mortal lives, attain to lasting truth and enduring significance only by being evaluated according to the divine measure. The story of his life in his twenties as he unfolds it, the story of the young aesthete, the budding author and the all-too-successful orator, is the tale of one who was in the business of "gaining the whole world", while at the same time "suffering the loss of his own soul" (Lk 9:25). Both the gain and the loss can be traced in the account which Augustine gives of his former friendships.

VI   Postscript: The 'Carthage Passage' in St Aelred of Rievaulx
It was in the first place through reading the *De Amicitia Spirituali* of St Aelred of Rievaulx, a good number of years ago, that I first learned to interpret the 'Carthage passage' along the lines I have unfolded here. In the third book of his dialogue Aelred at last opens his mind to his fellow-Cistercian and friends, the monks Walter and Gratian, concerning the deepest kind of friendship, namely that which takes as its model the words spoken by Jesus in John 15:15. Walter reacts at once. (In this dialogue his interventions frequently have the effect of reducing spiritual teaching to something commonsense, or even commonplace). Walter means to bring his abbot back from his spiritual flights and down to earth with a thud, when he interjects:

> The friendship you have just described is so sublime and perfect that I have not the courage to aspire after it. Gratian and I will be quite satisfied with the friendship described by your Augustine, which consists in conversing and laughing together, doing favours for one another...

and the 'Carthage passage' is quoted in full.[36] Walter's words follow it:

> This, according to our idea, is the attractive thing about friends, and we should feel qualms of conscience if we did not repay, with love, the affection showered on us by another. (This is an adaptation of the opening lines of *Conf.* IV.x.15).

Aelred's answer is forthright, even impatient: "Amicitia haec carnalium est, et maxime adolescentium."

> This is the type of friendship fostered by earthly-minded people — mostly callow youths — such as St Augustine and his friend were at the time he was speaking of. Still, provided it is free from anything unpleasant, it may be tolerated as the beginning of something more solid and sensible. With riper experience and a more spiritual outlook, with a deepening of the religious spirit and a zeal for the things of God, a youthful friendship may develop into something nobler and more sublime, just as friendship with man may eventually be transformed into friendship with God. Such a thing is possible on account of the likeness between them.

With these words he passes on to examine how spiritual friendship is to be cultivated.

In Aelred we can admire a spiritual man, one who is "the judge of all things" (cf. I Cor 2:15), and of friendship in particular. Walter, who was his medical doctor in life and who became his biographer (or rather, hagiographer), tells us that in the little oratory attached to the abbot's cell Aelred kept only three books, which towards the close of his life sufficed for his requirements: a glossed Psalter, the *Confessions* of St Augustine and the Gospel according to St John.[37] The abbot's familiarity with the Augustinian work is, we submit, impressively attested by his interpretation of the 'Carthage passage' on friendship.

---

[36] *Christian Friendship. By St Ailred of Rievaulx.* Trs., Hugh Talbot (London, 1942), p. 98. I have adapted Talbot's version slightly. For the critical edition see *Aelredi Rievallensis Opera Omnia*, CCCM I (Turnhout, 1971), *De Spirituali Amicitia* 85-87, pp. 335-336.
[37] *The Life of Ailred of Rievaulx by Walter Daniel.* Translated with Introduction and Notes by F.M. Powicke (London, 1950), p. lxv.

THE ETHICS OF PLOTINUS[1]

Kieran McGroarty

I   Plotinus and Porphyry's *Life*

The theme of this paper is, what I believe to be, the inconsistency in the life lived by Plotinus and the ethical teaching of the *Enneads*. This paper will do little more than set out the problem. We know quite a bit about the life Plotinus lived because of a biography written by his most famous pupil, Porphyry. We have some fragments from another biography by Eunapius and other bits and pieces. But Porphyry is the chief source.[2] We are lucky to have anything at all when we consider the opening lines of Porphyry's biography:

> Plotinus, the philosopher of our times, seemed ashamed of being in the body. As a result of this state of mind he could never bear to talk about his race or his parents or his native country (*Vita Plotini* 1.1-2).

This is the man who refused to sit for a portrait artist or sculptor because he saw little point in producing an image of what was only an image anyway (*VP* 1.7-9). They were reduced to passing off a portrait artist as a student in order to obtain a portrait of the great man. So to be Plotinus' biographer was, one imagines, no easy task. We speculate that Plotinus was born in Lycopolis (modern Assuit), on the banks of the Nile in Upper Egypt in A.D. 205.[3] We get his place of birth from Eunapius[4] not Porphyry. Plotinus's name is certainly Roman but he was most probably a Greek or at least from a Hellenized Egyptian family. His language was certainly Greek.

---

[1] This is the text of a paper presented as the first lecture in the Gerard Watson Memorial Series. It was written for an undergraduate audience who knew next to nothing about Plotinus. The text has been altered slightly, but, by and large, it reads as it was delivered. A much shorter version of this paper has appeared in the *Maynooth University Record*, 2000.

[2] As Armstrong rightly points out it is hard to see what there was that would have been available to Eunapius that was not available to Porphyry: Loeb Vol.1 (2nd edn.) pp. 2-3, footnote 1.

[3] On this see Rist, J.M., *Plotinus:The Road to Reality*, p. 248 footnote 8 and the references given there.

[4] Eunapius, *V. Soph.* (p. 6 Boissonade).

We know that he only turned to philosophy at the age of twenty-seven. He then set out for Alexandria where Porphyry tells us the teachers of philosophy had the highest reputations. After searching and discarding various teachers he settled down under the tutorship of Ammonius Saccas (*VP* 3.11ff.). If we know little about Plotinus we know a great deal less about Ammonius.[5] *"ein großer Schatten"* 'a greater shadow' he was called in a famous phrase by W. Theiler.[6] Ammonius Saccas wrote nothing and indeed Plotinus and two other of Ammonius's pupils (Erennius and Origen) agreed not to reveal his philosophy even after his death. This vow was however eventually broken,[7] which leaves us today trying to reconstruct his teachings from the writings of his pupils. Whatever it was that he was preaching it certainly caught the attention of Plotinus. Porphyry tells us that he:

> acquired so complete a training in philosophy that he became eager to make acquaintance with the Persian philosophical discipline and that prevailing among the Indians (*VP* 3.14-17).

In 242[8] he took part in the expedition of the Roman emperor Gordian III to the East. Gordian III had been saluted emperor by the Praetorian Guard at the age of 13. The Praetorian Prefect ran the emperor's affairs and set out on this expedition in reply to a Persian attack the previous year. There were substantial successes at first. Then Gordian was murdered in Mesopotamia in 244 through the machinations of Philip the Arab. The expedition ended in failure and Plotinus barely escaped with his life. He made his way to Antioch before finally settling in Rome at the age of 40 when Philip had become emperor.

Plotinus set up a school here and began teaching but at first he kept to the vow that he had taken regarding the teachings of Ammonius. The agreement was then broken by one of the other pupils and while Plotinus still wrote nothing down he began more and more to base his lectures on his studies with Ammonius (*VP* 3.33-34). But for ten years he wrote nothing down. Then in the tenth year of the reign of the emperor Gallienus

---

[5] See Schroeder, F., 'Ammonius Saccas', *Aufsteig und Niedergang der römischen Welt*, pp. 493-525.
[6] 'Plotin und die antike Philosopie', *Museum Helveticum,* 1, p. 215.
[7] See O'Brien, D., 'Plotinus and the Secrets of Ammonius', pp. 117-153.
[8] All dates are A.D.

Porphyry arrived in Rome. Plotinus was 59 years old by this time. Unfortunately everything noteworthy tends to happen after the arrival of Porphyry, or so Porphyry himself suggests, therefore we have to read him very carefully. One major event however did happen before Porphyry's arrival; that is, Plotinus had begun in 253 to write down the material that came up in discussion at the school. By the time of Porphyry's arrival in 263 Plotinus had completed 21 treatises. At Porphyry's urging Plotinus wrote another 24 treatises while Porphyry was with him. Needless to say Porphyry is inclined to think that this was his best work. So the total in 266 was 45 treatises. At that point Porphyry wasn't feeling the best and took himself off to Sicily to recuperate. While he was in Sicily Plotinus wrote the final nine treatises that have come down to us as the *Enneads*. A total of 54, 6 multiplied by 9, hence the title, *Enneads* (Nines).

By now Plotinus was in fairly poor health. Porphyry was not present but was informed about the lead up to Plotinus's death by those who stayed with Plotinus to the end, notably Eustochius. His voice lost its clearness, his sight became blurred and his hands and feet became ulcerated. He left the city and went to Campania to stay in the house of an old friend who had passed away. He died in 270.

To some extent those are the just the bare facts concerning his life and death. But Porphyry does also give us a good picture of the daily life of the philosopher and of Plotinus as an ordinary man surrounded by friends and involved in the same ordinary difficulties as everyone else. He had friends ranging from the emperor Gallienus and his wife Salonina to the ordinary people with whom he lived. Presumably some of these cared little for philosophy. He clearly did not live the sort of life one might associate with a mystic. Quite surprising is the fact that, according to Porphyry, he ran a sort of orphanage:

> Many men and women of the highest rank, on the approach of death, brought him their children, both boys and girls, and entrusted them to him along with all their property, considering that he would be a holy and god-like guardian (*VP* 9.5-9).

So he looked after other people's property when it was entrusted to him and took care that *he was accurate in such matters*[9] (*VP* 9.13-14). He was clearly not regarded as a philosopher who spent his time in some sort of mystic trance. The Aristophanic caricature of the philosopher in *Clouds* finds no place in Porphyry's *Life* of Plotinus. On the contrary, Plotinus appears to have lived a very ordinary life. He mixed with other people, greeting them intimately if we are to judge from Porphyry's note that when he developed leprosy his friends avoided him because he had the habit of greeting them by word of mouth (τὸ ἀπὸ στόματος...προσαγορεύειν) (Arm. tr.) (*VP* 2.16-17). He took his annual summer holiday from his job as a philosopher when he would only converse about ordinary everyday matters (ἄγοντος ἀργούς) (*VP* 5.4). He was by no means an intellectual snob. While it would be unfair to say perhaps that he suffered fools gladly, he clearly accepted that people had limitations (*VP* 7.7).

The Plotinus that emerges from Porphyry's *Life* is thus hard to reconcile with the philosopher of the *Enneads*. In *Ennead* III. 2 [47] 8. 16-21 we are asked:

> If some boys, who have kept their bodies in good training, but are inferior in soul to their bodily condition because of lack of education, win a wrestle with others who are trained neither in body or soul and grab their food and their dainty clothes, would the affair be anything but a joke?

Yet his own actions tell us that he clearly regarded the everyday difficulties of life as a serious affair for the non-philosopher. Those who had not yet taken or who were highly unlikely ever to take the 'upward path' he still protected from the day to day difficulties of ordinary life to the best of his ability (*VP* 9.16ff.). Porphyry strengthens this view of him by telling us that "he was gentle" (*VP* 9.18)[10] and that kindliness shone out from him (ἡ πραότης διέλαμπε) (*VP* 13.8-9). He was, we are told at the "disposal of *all* who had any sort of acquaintance with him" (*VP* 9.19-20).[11]

---

[9] My italics.
[10] See also *VP* 23.1ff.
[11] Armstrong tr., my italics.

Conversely he was clearly not averse to making use of a friend if the need arose. The emperor Gallienus and his wife Salonina greatly respected Plotinus. In return, Plotinus, in his quest to have Platonopolis established, tried to make full use of their friendship (*VP* 12.3). Here was a man who had a surprising degree of penetration into character (*VP* 11.1). He was worldly enough to notice that Porphyry had become suicidal and showed great *common* sense in advising a simple holiday as a remedy (*VP* 11.11ff.). He was, it seems, quite active in everyday affairs and obviously sufficiently self-possessed to the extent that even though he managed to spend twenty-six years in Rome and acted as an arbitrator in very many people's disputes, he never made an enemy of any of the officials (*VP* 9.20-22).

The question is this: how do we reconcile the philosopher of the *Enneads* with the man that emerges from Porphyry's *Life*? To understand why this is a problem we need to look briefly at the content of the *Enneads*. In particular we need to understand the metaphysical structure that underpins the ethics and the psychology of the *Enneads*.

II   The Metaphysical Structure of the *Enneads*
The first thing that should be made clear is that Plotinus differed greatly from Plato in one major respect. Plotinus was a *mystic*. Not only did he believe in a metaphysical construct designed to reveal another level of reality, as for example with Plato's Forms, he also believed that the philosopher was actually capable of making an ascent to the highest point in this other world. In fact Porphyry claims that Plotinus actually made such an ascent on four occasions:

> ...for his end and goal was to be united to, to approach the God who is over all things. Four times while I was with him he attained that goal (*VP* 23.15ff.).

At the top of Plotinus' hierarchical structure of reality is the *One*. The One is the undiminished giver from which all else comes. It produces, as all perfect things do, and what is produced is the world of Intellect. Intellect is the One in multiplicity, in multiplicity because being less perfect than the One it cannot retain its unity. This is the world of Plato's *Forms* and Aristotle's *Nous*. This is real Being; the One is beyond Being. Intellect too produces; the result of its production is Soul. This is a further remove from the unity and perfection of the One. Soul's attempt to express the multiplicity of Intellect results in the sense world that we have around us. This sensible world is merely an imperfect copy of the Intelligible world. As it is a lesser level it must operate in time not eternity. This sensible world is the home of the body/soul compound, that is, the human being. The important point is however, that soul is ultimately an inhabitant of the Intelligible world. It stretches from there to this sensible world which it has created. It is a bridge between the Intelligible and Sensible world. Important for us to understand, in view of the theme of this paper, is the fact that we, as body/soul compounds have a part of our soul that belongs to the Intelligible world. There is a part of our soul that never descends. This higher soul is always available to us if we choose to become conscious on its level. That is what the *Enneads* are instructing us to do.

There we have in a very brief and crude way Plotinus's metaphysical world.[12] I am well aware that I have given a fairly simple and uncontroversial account. What is clear though and free from dispute is the fact that we as human beings have our origins at a higher level and can return to that level if we choose. The world just described exists not only outside of the human being but also within us. The different metaphysical levels are not cut off from one another, rather the different levels of Being are traversed by the soul and the upward path is always at hand. We heard Porphyry say that Plotinus took this path four times while he was with him. He joined in mystical union with the One. Porphyry himself claims one such ascent. We can hear from Plotinus himself exactly what such an ascent was like:

> Often I have woken up out of the body to my self and have
> entered into myself, going out from all other things; I have seen
> a beauty wonderfully great and felt assurance that then most of
> all I belonged to the better part; I have actually lived the best life
> and come to identity with the divine; and set firm in it I have
> come to that supreme actuality, setting myself above all else in
> the realm of Intellect. Then after that rest in the divine, when I
> have come down from Intellect to discursive reasoning, I am

---

[12] One of the best general introductions to the metaphysics of the *Enneads* is still, in my opinion, the chapters in A.H. Armstrong, *An Introduction to Ancient Philosophy*, pp. 175-196.

25

puzzled how I ever came down, and how my soul has come to be in the body (*Ennead* IV. 8 [6] 1.1ff.).

You can see the basic Platonic idea of our souls belonging to a higher world but for some reason becoming ensnared in the material sphere. Why we come down is another matter that could be debated. But this metaphysical structure contains all the essentials. We have the freedom to leave the sensible world if we choose. Thus the duty of the philosopher is, as it was for Plato, to break out of that tomb which is the body and regain our proper metaphysical level. This is the stated objective of the Plotinian sage.

III   The Ascent

Since the One is within us, our efforts should tend towards an internal spiritual journey. The body, if not evil, is simply something that has attached itself to our lower soul, and so should be ignored as much as possible. It cannot be ignored completely:

> He must give to this bodily life as much as it needs and he can, but he is himself other than it and free to abandon it...(*Ennead* I. 4 [46] 16.17-18).

It is clear that the focus must be on the ascent to the Divine. This is in keeping with the Greek philosophical tradition to which Plotinus belonged. For Plato the objective was to become like God (*Theaetetus* 176b). Aristotle in the *Nicomachean Ethics* begins Book 1 by asking what is it that everyone strives after. The answer he arrives at is *eudaimonia*. This is not simply happiness but rather the highest and best possible life for a human being. This consists in the contemplation of God:

> ...but we ought so far as in us lies, to put on immortality, and to do all that we can to live in conformity with the highest that is in us... (1177b31ff.).

The philosophy of the *Enneads* is in general agreement with these views. But how exactly do we accomplish this? How do we break out of the body? Here Plotinus certainly goes beyond Plato. Plato advised the philosopher to pay as little attention to the body as possible while imprisoned in it and be unconcerned at having to abandon it. If he were to do that then he could sit with the smugness of Socrates in the *Phaedo*.

26

I can't persuade Crito that I am this Socrates here who is talking to you now and marshalling all the arguments; he thinks that I am the one whom he will see presently lying dead; and he asks how he is to bury me!...No you must keep up your spirits and say that it is only my body that you are burying; and you can bury it as you please... (*Phaedo*, 110d ff.).

In Plotinus the instructions are clear. We must, Plotinus tells us, take the upward path. We must strive to *bring back the god in us to the Divine in the All*.[13] We are souls who have chosen to desert the level of Intellect and live in the world of images that is this sense world. We *are* whatever conscious-level we choose to operate on. We can choose to be beguiled by the images that come from the sense world thinking them to be real and so spend our time being concerned with the body. We have also the option of ignoring the images that come to us from sense objects and the freedom to choose to focus on the realities of Intellect itself. We are, in a wonderful phrase by E.R. Dodds, "a fluctuating spotlight of consciousness."[14]

The *Enneads* are a handbook designed to help one make this mystical ascent, to help one become conscious on the level of Intellect, and there, to make contact with the One. This we can do. So becoming God-like is bound up with consciousness. How does one become conscious at the level of the higher soul? Plotinus tells us:

There are two stages of the journey for all, one when they are going up and one when they have arrived above. The first leads from the regions below, the second is for those who are already in the intelligible realm and have gained their footing There... (*Ennead* I. 3 [20] 1. 13ff.).

Plotinus then in this treatise termed *On Dialectic* by Porphyry, goes on to describe what sorts of things the ordinary aspirant should pay attention to and what steps s/he should follow. In fact the road he describes is very similar to the one so beautifully described by Plato in that wonderful piece in the *Symposium* where Plato outlines the ascent to the Form of Beauty.[15]

---

[13] *VP* 2.26
[14] Dodds, E.R., *Les Sources de Plotin*, pp. 385-386.
[15] *Symposium* 209e 5ff.

Part of the background training for this is the four cardinal virtues laid out in the Plato's *Republic*: Courage, Wisdom, Temperance, and Justice? So what sort of a person does the sage become?

IV   Ethics: Theory and Practice

One would assume that s/he would be quite indifferent to the matters of daily life. The only genuine help that the sage could give would be to turn those who are capable of it into philosophers and prepare them to become conscious on the level of real Being. One would assume from the *Enneads* that the sage would hardly bother with non-philosophers. What could s/he do for them? It is hard to see the sage then as a friend to all. This has indeed been the view of a number of scholars.[16] The most recent has been Dillon. He suggests with regard to the Plotinian sage:

> All earthly concerns such as love for family or kin, not to mention care for the poor and oppressed, and all passions, such as pity or grief, must be shaken off (like clothes at an initiation ceremony) in the process of purification.[17]

He also adds:

> One feels of Plotinus that he would gladly have helped an old lady across the road - but he might very well fail to notice her at all, and if she were squashed by a passing wagon he would remain quite unmoved.[18]

This is a reasonable comment to make based on the philosophy expounded in the *Enneads*. For instance in *Ennead* I. 2 [19] 7. 19-27 Plotinus has this to say:

> Perhaps the possessor of the [civic] virtues will know them, and how much he can get from them, and will act according to some of them as circumstances require. But when he reaches higher principles and different measures he will act according to these.

---

[16] See Plass, P., 'Plotinus' Ethical Theory', p. 253 and Westra, L., *Plotinus and Freedom*, p. 127.

[17] Dillon, J., 'An ethic for the late antique sage', p. 320.

[18] *Ibid.* p. 324.

For instance, he will not make self control consist in that former observance of measure and limit, but will altogether separate himself, as far as possible, from his lower nature *and will not live the life of the good man which civic virtue requires.*[19] He will leave that behind, and choose another, the life of the gods: for it is to them, not to good men that we are to be made like.

The point that I want to make is that I do not see how Plotinus the philosopher who espouses this philosophy in the *Enneads* can be easily reconciled with Plotinus the man as he appears in Porphyry's *Life*.[20] The problem is this: the imperative of the *Enneads* is that we must try to bring back the god in us to the divine in the All (*VP* 2.26). This would, one imagines, demand a somewhat reclusive lifestyle for the sage. This does not seem to be the lifestyle that emerges from Porphyry's biography. Indeed, I am not the only one who has found the philosophy of the *Enneads* slightly at odds with the philosopher evoked by the pen of Porphyry.

In 1984 Ferwerda[21] had this to say:

> But deep in our heart we cannot help remembering how Porphyry tells us that Plotinus was a very nice person, a man who showed a great deal of concern for what happened to other people. Does this not indicate a certain dichotomy between doctrine and behaviour?

More recently Bussanich[22] has noted:

---

[19] My italics

[20] It is by no means easy to see why A.H. Armstrong should conclude that " ..Plotinus was a complete and consistent character in whom life and thought were so closely related that it is not easy to understand the one without knowing something about the other." *The Cambridge History of Later Greek and Early Medieval Philosophy*, p. 3. Note too the same uneasy compromise in the philosophy of Epicurus. Epicureans were famous for their friendship but it is not easy to see why this should be so given their ethical philosophy that aimed at invulnerability.

[21] Ferwerda, R., 'Pity in the Life and Thought of Plotinus', p. 58.

[22] Bussanich, J., 'The Invulnerability of Goodness: The Ethical and Psychological Theory of Plotinus', p. 182.

Plotinus seems committed to the contradictory position that the philosopher will, on the one hand, be self-sufficient, free of constraining emotional attachments, and fully immersed in contemplation and, on the other hand, that she will also act virtuously and be friendly.

Bussanich logically goes on to ask how the biographical details of Plotinus' life can be reconciled with his metaphysical psychology.[23]

This was a man who looked after orphans. A man who patiently attended to the accounts of those who entrusted him with their property and *took care that they should be accurate* (*VP* 9.13ff). Porphyry says that he was gentle and at the disposal of all who had any sort of acquaintance with him (*VP* 9.19). Clearly he was not uncaring in any normal sense of the word. How do we reconcile this apparent ambiguity?

This is not a recent problem. As early as 1967 Rist had found difficulty with Plotinus' theory and practice. Given the metaphysics and psychology of the *Enneads* it is hard to see why the sage would bother with anyone else. Rist suggests that the only real help the philosopher could offer his friends is to demonstrate in his own life that the philosophic ascent is "possible and worthwhile".[24]

The theory of the self-sufficiency of the sage *should* preclude him from all communal interests....In theory the sage's only concern should be with teaching; in practice Plotinus both teaches those who can be taught and helps those who are not able to enter upon the path of philosophy so that they may avoid troubles which (in theory) are illusory in any case.[25]

Given the metaphysics and psychology of the *Enneads* it is hard to see why the sage would bother with anyone at all. As the quote above indicates, one could possibly argue that the only real help a philosopher could give is to teach.[26] But as Rist then observes: why bother even to teach? For Plotinus

---

[23] *Ibid.*
[24] Rist, J.M., *Road to Reality*, p. 163.
[25] See also Rist, J.M., 'Plotinus and Moral Obligation', pp. 217-233.
[26] Rist, J.M., *Road to Reality*, p. 163.

all that should matter is his own successful career of contemplation.[27] Rist says that there is no answer to this question in the *Enneads* and he suggests that we should not expect one.[28] But surely we are entitled to consistency between a life lived and a philosophy preached?

Rist does however offer a solution to the problem of why the sage might teach:

> There is a harmony in the whole of the universe. All things derive from the One and are, in Plotinus' language, in the One. All souls are striving to greater or lesser degrees to return to him. When any individual soul returns and is joined in communion with its source, it must be presumed to share in its source's creativity and causal energy. In other words, each soul will become responsible in its way for the creation and maintenance of all things. It will even love all things in so far as all things contain the principle of unity, for the One loves itself both in itself and in the rest of the cosmos.
>
> We know that the return of the soul is to be explained by the principle of 'like to like'. The soul is like the One, and the more it is purified the more it resembles the One's simplicity. Hence even before it achieves the union with its source which it seeks, it will be trying to act in a manner appropriate to the One. It will be sharing the One's omnipresence in so far as it can, and it will always be turned towards others, knowing that once they turn towards the One, they will be led back on the path to union. What higher motive could prompt a man to teach?[29]

This seems to me a reasonable argument as to why the sage would teach. It takes account of the metaphysics and psychology of the *Enneads*. But what about those who would or could not be taught? What responsibility does the sage have to these? None, one would imagine. Yet in practice Plotinus cared for these too. Rist traces this back to a fundamental problem in Plato:

---

[27] *Ibid.*
[28] *Ibid.*
[29] *Ibid.* pp. 163-164.

We may conclude therefore that just as Plotinus admitted the beauty of the visible world, while still holding it to be an 'unreal' beauty, so he admitted that practical help should be given to one's fellow humans while at the same time supposing that the problems that he was helping to solve were unreal problems. Thus if he ever supposed that it was not the philosopher's concern to act in such matters, he was as good as saying that the lesser goods of the visible world were no goods at all. We should recall at this point that he is undoubtedly the victim of Plato's divided thoughts on these problems. Is the true philosopher the dualistically-minded ascetic of the *Phaedo* or the interested dissector of the marvels of the visible world of the *Timaeus*?[30]

Having moved back to Plato, Rist suggests that the edict of the Cave in *Republic* may be the solution. Does Plotinus recognise a duty to his fellow humans? Was Plotinus following the command of Plato to go back into the Cave? Rist dismisses this because in his view the virtues for Plotinus, at their highest level, are purely contemplative. We do not go back into the Cave out of a sense of duty.[31] Aware that the problem has still not been solved Rist offers a final solution. He tells us that:

> ...in practice he [Plotinus] has recognised that concern for others does not entail the withdrawal of the mind from higher things and its submergence in the lower. The Plotinian soul is a subtle instrument; it can contemplate the higher and care for the lower at the same time.[32]

Metaphysically Rist is correct here. The sage *can* do this but the question still remains: why would the sage bother with the non-philosopher? Bussanich too offers a solution:

> In the special case of the philosopher, virtuous actions are accomplished spontaneously and easily; without feelings, deliberation, or choice; without awareness of the particulars; and

---

[30] *Ibid.* p. 166.
[31] *Ibid.*
[32] *Ibid.* p. 168.

with complete detachment as to the outcome (I.4.10.22-34, IV.4.8.4ff.).[33]

This explanation can, it seems to me, be drawn very reasonably from Plotinus's metaphysics but does not fully account for the picture of the sage delivered by Porphyry. Plotinus does not come across as an automaton, as someone without feelings. Although both Rist and Bussanich present Plotinus as someone operating on two levels, as he undoubtedly did, this does not, in my opinion, solve the problem. They tell us *what* the sage can do but they do not tell us *why* s/he would do it. We are still left with the question: why does the sage bother with the non-philosopher? I noted above that Rist had suggested that there is no answer in the *Enneads* to why the sage would bother with the non-philosopher. He may well be right. The philosophy of the *Enneads* is for specialists. The content is aimed at helping the philosopher achieve union with the One. It is not concerned with the non-philosopher.[34] But the *Enneads* also tell us that the sage has concerns for ordinary folk. At I. 4 [46] 11.13 we are told: "He would like *all men* to prosper and *no one* to be subject to any sort of evil",[35] imaginary or not one presumes. This is certainly reflected in Plotinus' life.

The answer to this problem may well lie in Plotinus' metaphysics. The creator of the sensible world, the World Soul, as Plotinus calls it, instinctively looks after its creation. And we are encouraged in the *Enneads*, as Smith[36] points out, to act like the World Soul. If we do, Smith suggests that "the norms of ethical conduct flow automatically and without difficulty from the higher life of Intellect."[37] The solution to this problem may well be along these lines, but the matter is, at least to me, still far from clear.

Bibliography

Armstrong, A.H., (ed.), *Plotinus* 7 vols., Loeb Classical Library, (Cambridge, Mass.: Harvard University Press, 1966-1989).

---

[33] Bussanich, J., *opt.cit.* p. 183.
[34] Smith, A., *Porphyry's Place in the Neoplatonic Tradition*, pp. 71,139.
[35] Armstrong translation.
[36] Smith, A., 'The Significance of Practical Ethics for Plotinus' in *Traditions of Platonism*, edited by J. Cleary, Aldershot: Ashgate Publishing Limited, 1999, pp. 234-235.
[37] Ibid, p.236.

———, *An Introduction to Ancient Philosophy* (London: Methuen, 1957). See pp. 175-196.

———, (ed.), *The Cambridge History of Ancient Philosophy* (Cambridge: CUP, 1967), pp. 195-268.

Bussanich, J., 'The Invulnerability of Goodness: The Ethical and Psychological Theory of Plotinus, *Proceedings of the Boston Area Colloquium in Ancient Philosophy*, vi (1990) pp. 151-184.

Dillon, J., 'An ethic for the late antique sage' in Gerson, L.P., *The Cambridge Companion to Plotinus* (Cambridge: CUP, 1996) pp. 315-335.

Dodds, E.R., *Les Sources de Plotin* Entretiens Hardt V, (Geneva,1960).

Ferwerda, R., 'Pity in the Life and Thought of Plotinus' in Runia, D.T., (ed.) *Plotinus amid Gnostics and Christians* (Amsterdam: Free University Press, 1984) pp. 53-72.

McGroarty, K., 'Plotinus on Eudaimonia' in McGroarty, K. (ed.) *Neoplatonica: Studies in the Neoplatonic Tradition* (Dublin: Hermathena, CLVII, 1994), pp. 103-115.

O'Brien, D., 'Plotinus and the secrets of Ammonius' in McGroarty, K., (ed.) *Neoplatonica: Studies in the Neoplatonic Tradition* (Dublin: Hermathena, CLVII, 1994).

Plass, P., 'Plotinus' Ethical Theory' *Illinois Classical Studies* 2 (1982), pp. 241-259.

Rist, J., *Plotinus: The Road to Reality* (Cambridge: CUP, 1967).

———, 'Plotinus and Moral Obligation' in R. B. Harris (ed.), *The Significance of Neoplatonism* (Norfolk, Va.: International Society for Neoplatonic Studies, Old Dominion University, 1976) pp. 217-233.

Schroeder, F.M., 'Ammonius Saccas', in Hasse and Temporini (eds.) *Aufsteig und Niedergang der römischen Welt* II 36.I (Berlin and New York: De Gruyter, 1987) pp. 493-526.

Smith, A., *Porphyry's Place in the Neoplatonic Tradition* (The Hague: Martinus Nijhoff, 1972).

Smith, A., 'The Significance of Practical Ethics for Plotinus', pp. 234-235 in *Traditions of Platonism*, ed. by J. Cleary, Aldershot: Ashgate Publishing, 1999.

Westra, L., *Plotinus and Freedom* (Lampeter: Edwin Mellen Press, 1989).

SENECA'S HINT OF POLITICAL DISSIDENCE

Maeve O'Brien

I   Introduction

The chorus of Argive Elders in Seneca's tragedy *Thyestes* is remarkably well informed about astrology.[1] The insertion of such apparent digressions as this was congenial to the reader steeped in rhetoric and integral to the literature of this so-called 'Silver Latin' period.[2] In addition, astrology fascinated almost everyone during the Neronian period, not least the emperor himself.[3]

---

[1] Seneca, *Thyestes*, 789-884. Thyestes' story was the subject of a Tragedy by Varius (29 BC), Quintilian *IO* X. i 98; the story is also told by Aeschylus, *Agamemnon,* 1517-1536; and in a lost play by Sophocles. The text of *Thyestes* used here is edited with introduction and commentary by R.J. Tarrant, (Scholars Press, American Philological Association, 1985). The most recent edition of the *Apocolocyntosis* is by R. Roncali, (Teubner, 1990). On authenticity and genre, see R. Brinckmann, 'Senecas' *Apocolocyntosis*' *ANRW* II 32, 2, pp. 884-914.

[2] A.J. Boyle (ed.), *The Imperial Muse: Ramus Essays on Roman Literature of the Empire,* (Berwick, 1988), and *ibid.*, 'Senecan Tragedy : Twelve Propositions', 79. Cf. Quintilian, *IO* IX i. 28, quoting Cicero, *De Oratore* III lii, 201: "Or we may employ digression and then, after thus delighting our audience, make a neat and elegant return to our main theme...". Also Quintilian, IX i. 35; ii. 55, and 66; iii 90. See G. Kennedy, *The Art of Rhetoric in the Ancient World* (Princeton, 1972), p. 116. Also M. Dewar, 'Laying it on with a trowel; the Proem of Lucan and related texts', *CQ* 44 (i) (1994), p. 199, I am in "the red faction". Digressions were used for the purposes of parody. Petr. *Sat.* 89, *Troia halosis*, in tragic iambic senarii, parodies sections of Seneca's *Agamemnon*; in *Sat.* 71, it is Seneca, *Ep. Mor.* 47; *Sat* 115, Seneca's *Consolatio ad Polybium* 9.6-7. Cf. J.P. Sullivan, 'On translating Petronius', in *Neronians and Flavians Silver Latin I,* edited by D.R. Dudley (London, 1972), pp. 172 and 182. Cf. M. Smith's edition, *Petronius' Cena Trimalchionis* (Oxford, 1975), p. 219, on the parallels between Seneca's letters and the *Satyricon.*

[3] The Trimalchio of Petronius' *Satyricon* knows more about astrology than almost anything else, *Satyricon,* 39 and 35. Compare his hilarious versions of the myths 50-52. *Thyestes* and *Satyricon* are very different in form. One is a tragedy, the other is a prose text not all of which is extant. R.G.M. Nisbet, 'The dating of Seneca's Tragedies, with special reference to *Thyestes*', *Papers of the Leeds International Seminar,* Sixth Vol. (1990), 95 (cf. p. 108), rejects the traditional dates in the forties for the tragedies and posits a date of A.D. 62 for *Thyestes*. See also, J.G. Fitch, 'Sense Pauses and Relative Dating in Seneca, Sophocles and Shakespeare', *AJP* 102 (1981), pp. 289ff. Cf. D. & E. Henry, *The Mask of Power: Seneca's tragedies and Imperial Rome* (Warminster, 1985), p. 9. Cf. K.F.C. Rose, (with an Introduction by J.P. Sullivan) *The Date and Author of the Satyricon* (Leiden, 1971), p. 74 'a *terminus post* of, say, mid-63 for the Cena...' Both

35

My purpose is to look at how Seneca comments indirectly and unfavourably on Nero in a rhetorical digression on the zodiac in a tragedy composed towards the end of Nero's reign. Here in *Thyestes*, Seneca uses the same astrological imagery to excoriate the experienced king Atreus that he had used to praise the young emperor Nero in a work composed at the very beginning of Nero's reign, the *Apocolocyntosis*. When Seneca is speaking of the crimes of kings in *Thyestes*, one eminent scholar maintains that at the most obvious level he is hinting less at the Julio-Claudians than the Arsacidae.[4] Nevertheless, he is hinting at Julio-Claudian Nero, and in a most uncomplimentary fashion.

II   Seneca, *Thyestes* 848-874

The order of the whole zodiac description in *Thyestes* mirrors and celebrates the order of the heavens which is soon to be no more.[5] *Cadere* is used three times in twenty-six lines, along with *excedere*. *Ire praeceps* and *ruere* frame the extract relevant to our purpose which is taken from the choral song.[6] This accords with Seneca's use of Stoic imagery: the universe in turmoil reflects the evil of the individual through the notion of *sympatheia*. The cosmic catastrophe motif, especially in relation to celestial collapse, is used to presage the ruin of the world.[7] This is also a very common Hellenistic motif, famously in Callimachus' *Lock of Berenice*. Astrological descriptions are common in Senecan tragedy, but none on so detailed a scale as that in *Thyestes,* where the sun falls and then the moon, followed by the stars of the zodiac and the circumpolar constellations.[8] In *Thyestes* this description of the collapse of the zodiac is all in the future tense and the whole choral ode is addressed to Apollo and Jupiter. But, by the end of the ode, the gods have left the scene and it appears that the stars

---

texts can plausibly be dated to the sixties of the first century, *Thyestes* to 62 and *Satyricon* to late 63, though there are few certainties in this debate.

[4] Nisbet (1990), p. 110 "Seneca....understood at first hand the temptations of power that ruined Thyestes, but he had not yet utterly despaired of Rome or his own position. When he speaks of the crimes of kings,...at the most obvious level he is hinting less at the Julio-Claudians than the Arsacidae."

[5] Tarrant (1985), p. 211.

[6] Sen. *Thy.* 848-874, Complete choral ode 789-884.

[7] Cf. T.G. Rosenmayer, *Senecan Drama and Stoic Cosmology* (Berkeley, 1989), p. 153.

[8] For example, Seneca, *Agamemnon* 486 ff. On intertextuality between *Agamemnon* and *Thyestes*, see A.J. Boyle (1988), p. 92.

have already fallen because of the actions of the king. Atreus announces that he himself is equal to the stars:

> Aequalis astris gradior et cunctos super
> altum superbo vertice attingens polum
> ...dimitto superos.

> Equal to the stars I proceed, touching with my haughty
> head the lofty sky over all....I dismiss the gods.

> (Sen. *Thy.* 885-886)

The commonplace of a person being equal to the stars is exploited so that the sentence can mean not only that Atreus sees himself as a god, but also that he has in some way brought the gods down to his level and degraded them.[9] And appropriately, he himself imperiously states that he has dismissed the gods. Though delivered in a play about a mythical and fictional king this is a political, and perhaps a potentially dangerous comment in an era of growing emperor-cult. Seneca was well aware of the assimilation Nero-Sol-Apollo since the earliest days of Nero's reign.[10]

III   Seneca, *Apocolocyntosis*

Now the comments about Atreus are even more dangerous when one observes that in the *Apocolocyntosis*, Phoebus calls Nero his equal, "my equal in song no less than voice" (*me cantu nec voce minor*).[11] Here Nero is spoken about specifically as being equal to a god and to the stars also because he is depicted as the good ruler.[12] Nero encouraged comparison of

---

[9] Cf. Tarrant (1985), p. 216.

[10] Cf. O. Weinreich, *Senecas Apocolocyntosis* (Berlin, 1923), p. 44.

[11] *Apoc.* 4.1.23, and P.T. Eden, Seneca: *Apocolocyntosis* (Cambridge, 1984), p. 34 and notes *ad loc*.

[12] Even though Nero is not called *rex* here, he is in *De Clementia*, where the good philosophical king is described. Cf. M.T. Griffin, *Seneca, A Philosopher in Politics* (Oxford, 1976), p. 147, with whom I agree, thinks that this may indicate that Seneca accepts that the principate is equivalent to a monarchy, and the best he can do is "infuse into the institution the qualities of ideal kingship to which all the philosophical schools paid tribute."

himself to the Sun with his commissioning of the colossus fashioned with his own face and which Vespasian later dedicated to Sol.[13]

Seneca subverts the sun imagery he used of the real Nero in the *Apocolocyntosis* when he uses the same imagery of fictional Atreus in the *Thyestes*. Indeed, the stars and sun imagery which is linked with the prospective good reign of Julio-Claudian Nero in the *Apocolocyntosis* acts as a subtext of *Thyestes* where the falling stars and sun are associated with the malign rule of the Pelopid house.

IV *Thyestes* and *Apocolocyntosis*
Observe the terms used to describe the young Nero in the *Apocolocyntosis* and the experienced Atreus in *Thyestes*.[14] For example, Apollo is present at the beginning of the young Nero's reign (*Phoebus adest. Apoc.* 4.15). Even though Atreus thinks he is equal to the stars (*aequalis astris*), even he realises that the sky is empty (*perge dum caelum vacat. Thy.* 892). In order to reinforce the point, the chorus remark that Phoebus has left the scene (*cur Phoebe tuos rapis aspectus? Thy.* 793). This suits Seneca's depiction of a world beset by the demands of pernicious government, a government which is epitomized in Atreus. Nero is compared to the morning star "scattering the stars in flight" (*qualis discutiens fugientia Lucifer astra. Apoc.* 4.25). Atreus asserts that even though the day be unwilling he will scatter (*discutiam*) the shades (*tenebras*) from around his poor brother, and he wishes that he could hold the stars now fleeing (*utinam quidem tenere fugientes deos*) so that Thyestes' miseries and his banquet of revenge become apparent.[15]

On the contrary, the young Nero will dispel shades and herald an era of prosperity. "He will guarantee an era of prosperity to the weary and break the silence of the laws" (*felicia lassis saecula praestabit legumque silentia rumpet. Apoc* 4. 30-33).[16] Nero is the bringer of light. This imagery is also evident in the phrase "Such a Caesar is now present" (*talis Caesar adest*),

---

[13] T. Barton *Ancient Astrology*, (London, 1994), p. 204.

[14] Both texts are also in verse metre; the relevant section of the *Apocolocyntosis* in simple epic hexameters, the speech of Atreus in iambic trimeters, while the chorus sings in anapaestic dimeters.

[15] 890-900 *passim*. Also sun's course reversed, *Thy.* 120-1, 789-880, 990-5.

[16] Cf. *De Clem.* 1.1.4 Seneca makes Nero say "...the laws which I have called out of neglect and the shadows..." and Eden (1984), p. 78.

recalling Phoebus' earlier presence (*Apoc.* 4.15.). The text continues in the future tense: "....such a Nero shall Rome now gaze upon. His radiant face blazes with gentle brilliance and his shapely neck with flowing hair" (...*talem iam Roma Neronem aspiciet. Flagrat nitidus fulgore remisso vultus et adfuso cervix formosa capillo. Apoc.* 4.30-33). The adjective *nitidus* is used especially of heavenly bodies.[17] The praise of Nero contrasts point for point with the vituperation applied to Atreus, and both accounts are expressed rhetorically using the stars of the zodiac.[18]

During the reign of Atreus, Phoebus is absent from the scene, the opposite will pertain in the reign of Nero. Atreus wishes to hold the night stars even though it is morning. This unnatural situation is reversed with Nero who scatters the night stars: Nero will dispel darkness and shade. Atreus wants to keep the darkness and shade around his brother. Nero is constantly the bringer of light whereas Atreus invites the darkness. This imagery of darkness and light and the same astrological references to stars and especially the light-giving Phoebus used in relation to Atreus illustrate the inevitability of the ruin he will draw down on humanity. This imagery and these references are used of Nero and the prospective good he will do, as seen by Seneca in the first months of his reign. Nero will shine as a star himself in the heavens equalling Phoebus.[19]

V   Seneca and kingship

What implications does this extraordinary coincidence of zodiac imagery have for Seneca's view of Nero's reign? Now, it is important to note here that in the imperial period the control of state religion including astrology fell gradually from the hands of the old ruling class of the republic to the

---

[17] Cf. Lucretius, *De Rerum Natura* I. 9; Virgil, *Georgics* I. 467; Martial, 8.21.9, an engaging poem about Domitian and the stars. *Fulgor* can be used of the sun or moon and concretely to mean a shining object such as a meteor.

[18] Cf. *Cambridge History of Classical Literature*, chapter 8, F.R.D. Goodyear, 'Prose Satire', p. 138 "...the praise of Nero can be taken seriously." Also Dewar (1994), p. 209. On the *topoi* involved in encomiums, "The Roman eulogist was clearly perfectly prepared to say ten impossible things before breakfast, but neither he, nor his honorand, nor his audience was expected to take them literally...But 'seriously' is a different matter."

[19] Atreus sees himself as the most exalted of heaven dwellers and king of kings, *Thy.* 911-13. He is not a shining example of a good king. Overly ambitious, he is characterized as greedy *avidus*, especially by means of animal imagery, 491 ff., compare 707ff., and 734. Cf. Greedy chaos in *Hercules Furens*, 677.

emperor.[20] This means that astrologers did not need to report publicly to the board of augurs, but privately to the emperor. Astrology became popular with everyone under the empire and this was especially the case with the emperor.[21] Nevertheless, if any ordinary person, or even a noble such as P. Anteius Rufus, sought to consult an astrologer on his own behalf, disastrous consequences were likely to ensue for the individual.[22] Astrology then became a tool of imperial authority and however rhetorically expressed any reference to astrology and kingship together in a work of literature was a loaded reference.

In Seneca's *Thyestes* the Chorus' description of the collapse of the stars, in which every sign of the zodiac is catalogued, is used to illustrate the pernicious rule of King Atreus.[23] Now, Nero encouraged comparison of himself to the sun god, Phoebus Apollo, because of his perception of his own talent as a charioteer and a singer.[24] For some years after Nero's death

---

[20] L.R. Taylor, *Party Politics in the Age of Caesar* (Berkeley, 1949), pp. 76 and 97.

[21] Barton, (1994), p. 63. Cf. P. Garnsey and R. Saller, *The Roman Empire : Economy Society and Culture*, (London, 1987), p. 178, "Following the victory of Augustus, institutions, values and cultural life in Rome gradually adjusted to the monarchy." Cf. J.H.W.G. Liebeschuetz, *Continuity and Change in Roman Religion* (Oxford, 1979), pp. 119-39; and 155-166, on religious anxiety and the fall of Nero.

[22] Tac. *Ann.* 16.14. V. Rudich, *Political Dissidence under Nero: The price of dissimulation* (London, 1993), p. 145, "It was no secret that not only the practice of astrology but even a mere request for a horoscope could easily result in a charge of magic and treason against the ruling emperor", and pp. 160-161 on the treason trial of Soranus and the trumped up charge of consulting an astrologer Nero concocted against his daughter, Servilia.

[23] Cf. E.J. Kenney (ed.), *The Cambridge History of Classical Literature* Vol. II part 4, article by C.J. Herington, 'The Younger Seneca', p. 33, "The major movement of the song is occupied by a surrealist vision of the collapse of the flaming constellations into chaos – its effects marred only by the fact that every sign of the zodiac is catalogued in detail." Also, D. & E. Henry (1985), p. 37, who surmise that the reason for such long, and to the modern ear, tiresome, passages replete with astronomical geographical and mythological detail is Seneca's insistence on the cosmic aspect of disorder.

[24] Suetonius, *Nero*, 25, and other gods 53; Dio, 61.20.5. On his passion for horse racing, Tac. *Ann.* 14.14.1; Dio, 62.15.1; 63.1.1. E.M. Smallwood, *Documents illustrating the Principates of Gaius Claudius and Nero* (Cambridge, 1967), no. 144, a coin from the mint of Rome, the radiate crown appears on the head of a living emperor, dates A.D. 64-66. Worship of the emperor was especially common in areas of Greek influence such as Campania, as seen in the so-called *Feriale Cumanum, CIL. x* 8375.

people left flowers on his grave and even had statues made of him which they put up on the rostra.[25]

The *Apocolocyntosis* which was produced for Nero's first Saturnalia about two months after he had become emperor in A.D. 54, shows Seneca's concern that Nero should govern well.[26] The structure is simple: the old emperor Claudius is at the point of entering into his eternal reward. He finds difficulty in doing so, and is not helped by Augustus' denunciation of him. Seneca offers an unfavourable satiric account of Claudius' stewardship of the empire, coloured one imagines by Seneca's unhappy experience under his regime.[27] A uniquely surviving specimen of Menippean Satire from the Roman world, the function of the work has been disputed, but apart from entertainment and the luxurious joy of getting his own back on Claudius, Seneca may also have sought to advise his young pupil, who was now the emperor, that this was not the way to govern.[28] In contrast to Claudius, the young emperor Nero is praised.

For these reasons, Seneca could not subsequently express open distaste for his former pupil's way of conducting the business of the empire, but he could in a covert way reverse all the good that he had openly said Nero would do as the future emperor by excoriating Atreus in exactly similar terms in *Thyestes*.

VI   Nero and Atreus
The story of Atreus and his brother was a favourite one with Nero, and Thyestes was actually one of the tragic roles played by Nero.[29] The emperor

---

[25] Suetonius, *Nero* 57; cf. *Ibid.*, *Otho*, 7; Dio, 64.6; Plutarch, *Otho*, 3; Tac. *Hist.*, I.4, 16 25, and 78; II 11.

[26] H. Furneaux, *Commentary*, Vol. II, 303, on 13.69.1; and Eden (1984), p. 5 n. 11. See also Griffin (1976), p. 129 and Goodyear, *Cambridge Hist.*, p. 137, regarding authorship, which is generally agreed (and also by me) to be Seneca.

[27] His exile (A.D. 41-48), due to presumed adultery with Julia Livilla. Cf. Dio, 60.8.5.

[28] Eden (1984), Introduction, p. 13. Cf. A. Momigliano (tr. W. Hogarth), *Claudius, the emperor and his achievement* (Cambridge, 1934, repr. 1961), p. 77. This message would have been agreeable to Nero in any case. Cf. CIL. xiv. 163, on the naming of the sea harbour at Rome *Portus Augusti* to deprive Claudius of the honour of giving his name to the work which he had started, Suetonius, *Claudius*, 20.

[29] Dio 63, 9. 4. Cf. Suetonius *Nero*, 21, Juvenal, *Sat* VIII 228ff. and Duff, *Comm.* 315. Also, K.R. Bradley, *Suetonius' Life of Nero: An Historical Commentary* (Brussels, 1978), p. 134.

has alarmingly for Seneca, just as alarmingly as an Atreus or a Thyestes, become a performer in the spectacles which he sponsors.[30] Suetonius emphasis that the emperor was also fond of acting as an *auriga* too, when Nero replaced the usual praetor and let one of his freedmen signal the beginning of a race in which the emperor took part.[31]

Atreus exemplifies an eastern type of king. He sees himself as the most exalted of the heaven dwellers and king of kings (*Thy.* 911-13, and 885ff.) and Nero is now similar in his old tutor's eyes. Nero's philhellenism and bias for things Eastern, not to mention the megalomania visible in him in the last two thirds of his reign, is surely comparable to Atreus as a king. For example, Dio describes the pomp and circumstance which attended the coronation of Tiridates, king of Armenia, in Rome in A.D. 66. It could not have been seen by Seneca but the preparations for it may have been.[32] Such was the magnificence and profusion of golden decorations in the theatre where the coronation took place that the people called the day itself golden. Significantly, the awning which blocked out the sun overhead was adorned with an embroidered figure of Nero driving a chariot, golden stars gleaming all about him.[33]

VII   Conclusion

The notion of the mortal ruler among the stars is familiar from Callimachean poetry especially the famous *Lock of Berenice* copied in Catullus 66. But the point of comparison between Nero and Atreus, along with the astrological light and darkness imagery and its subtle re-working,

---

[30] Cf. Nisbet (1990), pp. 102-3, Cf. M.T. Griffin, above in note 25. A.J. Boyle, *Hic epulis locus* : The tragic worlds of Seneca's *Agamemnon* and *Thyestes'*, p. 213, in *Seneca Tragicus: Ramus Essays on Senecan Drama* (Berwick, 1983). Cf. *Ibid.* (1988), p. 93. E.M. Smallwood, (1967), document no. 40, a dedicatory inscription from Lycopolis in Egypt invoking the good luck of Nero, similar to the honours given to Hellenistic monarchs. For other Hellenistic features, cf. Suet. *Nero*, 20.3 on the *Augustiani,* Nero's personal bodyguard and cheerleaders; 51, long hair, which is also characteristic of an *auriga.*

[31] Suet. *Nero*, 22, and Bradley (1978), p. 137. Also S. Bartsch, *Actors in the Audience* (Cambridge, Mass., 1994), p. 35, on the blurring boundaries between the reality of fiction of the audience and the actors on the stage during Nero's reign.

[32] Cf. Tac. *Ann.* 15. 29.1, and also 16. 23. 3; Dio, 63. 1. 1-2. Nero's philhellenism is ilustrated by the famous inscription, no. 64 (Smallwood, 1967) which refers to Nero's grant of 'freedom' to the province of Achaea in 67.

[33] Dio, 63.6.2.

show that Seneca has revised his opinion of Nero downwards so that Nero's erstwhile tutor has neatly reversed or even subverted this well known Hellenistic motif. Nero has not been an enlightening presence. *Satur est* says Atreus of Thyestes, but it could just as easily be said about Nero in A.D. 62 especially by Seneca, who was just then falling completely out of favour.[34]

---

[34] Cf. R. Syme, *Tacitus*, Vol. II (Oxford, 1958), 743, and among his replacements, T. Petronius Niger. Cf. M.T. Griffin (1976), 423.

PATRICK ON THE MARGINS OF SPACE AND TIME

Thomas O'Loughlin

I   Introduction

How do I see myself in space and time? This is not the sort of question most people pose to themselves consciously; indeed when space and time are thought of at all it is usually as sets of impersonal co-ordinates that form a grid relating locations and events. Time and space as an organising grid is all around us: an entry 'meeting, room x' against a line in a diary; 'I will see you next week'; "In the fourteenth year of King Hezekiah" (Is 36:1); 'I live near Dublin'; "In those days a decree went out from Caesar Augustus that all the world should be enrolled. ... when Quirinius was governor of Syria" (Lk 2:1-2); or the interesting 'Dublin and London are an hour's flight apart' where space is measured by time. In these examples the time and space grids are assumed to exist independently of the observers forming an objective frame against which changes can be reckoned. The extreme form of this occurs when we locate places/events against a frame that has a 'given' quality: "Dublin is 53°20'N 6°15'W." Such frames can now become almost absolutes in our thinking – dividing a circle into 360 units and the Greenwich meridian make them into more 'facts' to be respected. Likewise we produce clocks that are tied as closely as possible to the regularities in nature, and 'what they tell us'– presumably time – is perceived as another 'fact' rather than a mutually agreed inference.[1]

However, there is another space and time within which we exist. Individual to each of us, this personal sense of time and place, of its nature, is not public even when it is shared by many in a community or society. This is our private sense of *where* we are *now*. This private sense of time and space is often apprehended negatively. We have a sense of *how far away* certain events or places are from us. While we think of some events as long ago and almost forgotten, other events were 'pivotal,' and some happened 'at the wrong time.' We think of certain places as our own or 'familiar' (an interesting choice of word), other places as distant, strange, even alien. These personal notions of space and time are very hard to tie down – often we are barely conscious of them and we only externalise them, in ways that

---

[1] The contrast between modern and early medieval views of time is explored in my *Celtic Theology: Humanity, World and God in Early Irish Writings* (London, 2000), pp. 166-184.

others can glimpse, incidentally. Today they are frequently labelled 'mental maps' but the vagueness of the term is witness to the problems inherent in ascertaining these aspects of an individual's thought.[2] This is tantalising to the historian or biographer, as any glimpse will help in understanding his/her subject, but this insight can only be had by assembling numerous little pieces into a pattern, without a guarantee that the pattern is the correct sum of the parts. The best sources for these reconstructions are personal documents where public space and time do not predominate. Letters are the most common source, but autobiographical materials – diaries and the like – are perhaps those most likely to yield detailed results. If this is so, then the writings of Patrick are an obvious target for examination: the *Confessio* (hereafter *Conf.* with the customary section number) is explicitly autobiographical (even if we cannot be sure who is intended as the ideal reader: God, bishops in Britain, Christians in Ireland, or a combination) while the *Epistola militibus Corotici* (hereafter *Ep.* with the customary section number) is not only personal, but autobiographical in that Patrick is a central actor in the events which give rise to the letter and the threats it contains.[3]

---

[2] Cf. S. Gole, 'Important is Big!' in P. Barber and C. Board (eds)., *Tales from the Map Room* (London, 1993), pp. 16-17 which reproduces the anonymous map intended to portray the world of the 'Sloane Ranger' which captures the essence of 'private space': what is important equals what is significant within my world of values, contacts, and prejudices. On the question of how space is a personal phenomenon before it is a public, 'objective' one, cf. the collection of essays by J.Z. Smith in *Map is not Territory* (Leiden, 1978). The notion of 'mental map' appears to originate with J.E. Dornbach, 'The Mental Map,' *Annals of the Association of American Geographers* 49 (1959), pp. 179-180, but has now generated a vast literature, but two older works still provide the best introduction: K. Lynch, *The Image of the City* (Cambridge MA, 1960); and P. Gould and R. White, *Mental Maps* (Harmondsworth, 1974); while the collection of essays edited by D. Cosgrove, *Mappings* (London, 1999) gives several examples of how the concept has been taken over by other branches of the humanities apart from geographers. On the application of the notion of 'mental maps' to early medieval literary texts cf. my 'The View from Iona: Adomnán's Mental Maps,' *Peritia* 10 (1996) pp. 98-122; and my 'Maps and Acts: A Problem in Cartography and Exegesis,' *Proceedings of the Irish Biblical Association* 21 (1998) pp. 33-61.

[3] The edition used is, in the main, that of L. Bieler, *Libri Epistolarum Sancti Patricii Episcopi* (Dublin, 1952) – but bearing in mind the criticisms of M. Esposito, 'St Patrick's "Confessio" and the "Book of Armagh",' *Irish Historical Studies* 8 (1954), 1-12 – I occasionally use that of N.J.D. White (*Proceedings of the Royal Irish Academy* 25c7 (1905)) and note this. The translation of Patrick's writings is that of one of the honorands of this volume, as found in D. Conneely, *The Letters of Saint Patrick* (Maynooth, 1993), pp. 63-81. For the rationale for my not restricting myself to Bieler's edition, and for a full

That there should be yet another paper on the career of Patrick calls for some comment. Normally, personal senses of space and time are things very secondary to the historian – if they are mentioned at all. The ambition is to locate persons and events within a frame of space and time that is external to the actors, and as objective to the modern observer as possible. But there is a great irony here regarding Patrick: while in terms of the normal historical quest we have almost no certain dates or locations,[4] the sources do contain many clues as to his personal sense of time and place. As early as the seventh century no one really knew where Bannavem Taburniae (or is it 'Bannaventa Berniae'?[5]) was,[6] and the numerous attempts in this century to identify it have been no more successful.[7] The same is true of 'the wood of Foclut,' or his dates. The assault of Binchy,[8] despite a later mellowing of tone,[9] on all who would construct a 'history' of Patrick is decisive. So, on the one hand, the information that is usually the easiest to obtain is here beyond reach; but, on the other hand, that which eludes us in so many medieval sources is in Patrick's case at hand in relative abundance.

II   A Stranger

The most obvious clue to how Patrick saw his location is that it is 'among strangers.' Repeatedly he declares that he is away from home and an alien in Ireland. This sense of being apart appears as something quite acute: he

---

apparatus biblicus to Patrick – as will be used in this paper, see my *Saint Patrick: The Man and his Works* (London, 1999). All citations of scripture follow the Vulgate numeration, and all translations are my own.

[4] For a discussion of the evidence for dating Patrick, see *Celtic Theology*, pp. 25-30; and on the problematic of dating/locating him, see *Saint Patrick: The Man and his Works*, pp. 14-34.

[5] See D.R. Howlett, *The Book of Letters of Saint Patrick the Bishop* (Dublin, 1994), p. 52.

[6] Muirchú did not know its location; cf. *Vita Patricii* I, 1 (1) in L. Bieler ed., *The Patrician Texts in the Book of Armagh* (Dublin, 1979), p. 66.

[7] Suggesting locations for this place has been a specific sub-section of interest in Patrick. Places ranging from Cornwall, through Anglesey, to Carlisle, and some places even further away, have had their supporters; a survey of all these theories by Anthony Harvey is due to appear shortly in his bibliography of Patrick.

[8] D.A. Binchy, 'Patrick and his Biographers, Ancient and Modern,' *Studia Hibernica* 2 (1962), pp. 7-173.

[9] D.A. Binchy, 'A pre-Christian survival in medieval Irish hagiography,' in D. Whitelock, R. McKitterick, D. Dumville (eds), *Ireland In Early Medieval Europe* (Cambridge, 1982), pp. 165-78.

does not belong to this place or its people, and his home is not just across the sea in Britain (*Conf.* 23) but it is *far* away. The *Confessio* opens with a statement of where home is: Bannavem Taburniae. This is a place he knows well and identifies with, his family have deep roots there as members of the decurion/clergy class, and he expects the reader likewise to know the place, and recognise his family's social status (*Conf.* 1). Taken from home he suffers the consequences of not studying his own language and of having to express himself in an alien tongue (*in linguam alienam*) (*Conf.* 9). But this suffering is justified by its end: for he has been, and is, prepared "to hear the opprobrium of being a foreigner" (Sir 29:30) in order that he preach the gospel (Mk 13:10)[10] to the Irish (*Conf.* 37).

This juxtaposition of scriptural texts, Sirach and Mark,[11] is interesting for understanding him as a 'foreigner for the gospel.' Sirach 29:28-35 sets out the primary needs of a man for life and happiness. Basic to a happy life is living in one's own home with one's own family. Sirach asks "What are a man's first needs?" and replies that they are "Water, bread, clothing, and the safety of a *home*." Indeed, the poor man with a home is better than one living in the presence of splendour without one. The little man dwelling in his own home is far better off than the stranger wandering from house to house accepting hospitality. It is a bitter thing to be homeless and it invites one to be reviled. As long as you are *with your own people and in your*

---

[10] Patrick says that he came "to preach the gospels to the Irish peoples" (*ad Hibernas gentes euangelium praedicare*) (*Conf.* 37) while Mk 13:10 reads that "the gospel must be preached to all the nations" (*in omnes gentes primum oportet praedicari euangelium*). The change from the passive to the active voice may be significant given, as we shall see, Patrick's overall sense of fulfilling what is commanded about preaching in the gospels: Jesus spoke about what has to have taken place before the eschaton, Patrick is setting out to help in accomplishing this result.

[11] Patrick consciously set biblical texts in various relationships to one another in his writing; and this practice of producing a new theological picture from such textual mosaics is one of the few pointers he gives us to the nature of his sources. In *Epistola* 9 he refers to "the testimonies (*testimonia*) of the whole law" which probably refers to books of scriptural testimonies (verses put together to support particular doctrinal or moral points) such as the famous one of Cyprian, the *Testimonia ad Quirinum* (*CCSL* 3). These were complex theological tools rather than simple collections of 'favourite quotations,' but they are largely unknown to modern scholarship; for an introduction to these works and their use, cf. A.C. Sundberg, 'On testimonies,' *Novum Testamentum* 3 (1959), 268-81; and on their use cf. *Clauis Patrum Latinorum* (3e), n. 1019a; and T. O'Loughlin, 'The Text of Cyprian's *Ad Quirinum* III, LVIII: An Emendation,' *Manuscripta* 40 (1996) pp. 49-53. However, a search using the files of the Vetus Latina Institut (Beuron) to see if Patrick used any extant collection of *testimonia* has proven fruitless.

home (my emphasis is an attempt to reflect the force of Patrick's words) you do not have to hear the hatred that is heaped on the stranger (*et improperium peregrinationis non audies*). Sirach captures the sense of alienation felt by so many who have had to live as exiles or immigrants in a society which does not welcome them, and at the same time promotes the notion of home found in the rhyme: 'Be it ever so humble there's no place like home.' This whole passage from Sirach, not just the line Patrick quotes, seems to capture his sense of being a stranger where he is.

When, moreover, Sirach is read in combination with the statements of Christ on preaching from Mark, Patrick's self-portrait seems complete. In Mark the preacher of the gospel has to abandon home, brothers, sisters, mother, fathers, children, and his own fields (Mk 10:29); he suffers insults and is dragged before his own religious leaders in the synagogues and before foreign[12] kings and rulers (*praesides*) where he has to bear witness to Christ (Mk 13:9-10). So for Patrick to be a preacher is to be cut off from home and family, to have the lot of the suspect stranger, and to suffer the extremes of home sickness for he has no home in Ireland. In *Confessio* 37, Patrick's presentation of his experience seems to fit with this reading of the scriptures down to the last detail: grace (here presented as equivalent to the divine will), not himself, sent him to Ireland to preach, so he lives among strangers, endures insults from aliens (unbelievers), is taunted as a foreigner, treated as a prisoner, has heard hatred uttered against him, and endures many persecutions.

But this theme of suffering as a stranger is a recurring one. He repeatedly notes that he has left his parents (*Conf.* 23, 43, and *Ep.* 1), those he would like to have as friends (*Conf.* 43), and his homeland (*patria*) (*Conf.* 43 and *Ep.* 1) for the sake of the gospel. Indeed, he has given up his own estate (*uillula*) for his mission (*Conf.* 1) which echoes those in Mk 10 who have given up their own fields (*agri*) for the gospel. He has been held in contempt (*Conf.* 1), has had to forage for food (*Conf.* 22), and been despised (*Ep.* 1): these are the dangers Sirach sees facing the foreigner. He has been betrayed by those close to him (*Conf.* 32), has had plots hatched against him (*Conf.* 35), has been brought before his own religious leaders and rejected (*Conf.* 26-7, and 29), and brought before foreign kings (*Conf.* 52) and judges (*qui iudicant*) (*Conf.* 53); all these problems are consistent with what is foretold in Mk 13 for the preacher. And having been taken, in

---

[12] This is implied in that the preacher is also brought before the rulers of the synagogues.

his youth, as a captive to an alien land, he takes up again that slavery – and with it exile – in response to a divine call (*Conf.* 37, 43, and 61; and *Ep.* 10). The gospel's task alone, he tells us, explains his spending his life far from home and family (*Conf.* 61), for as a young man he was told to go home from there (*Conf.* 17) and later told to go back to preach (i.e. leave home once more) (*Conf.* 23). Implicit in these directions is that Ireland is an alien place and that Patrick dwells there among 'the nations' (*Conf.* 48). In the *Epistola* (11) this being without his home is presented as a basic quality of ministry founded directly on the teaching and experience of Christ: "a prophet has no honour in his own land" (Jn 4:44). While he quotes John, he has in mind an image of this text that is based on all the uses of this theme in the gospels (cf. Mt 13:57; Mk 6:4; Lk 4:24) for Patrick reads the phrase in its Synoptic context of rejection from homeland and family, and with it the duty to live as a stranger. This passage in the *Epistola*, when read against the related passages in the *Confessio*, shows Patrick as viewing his sense of alienation from home as part of the configuration of his own mind to the mind of Christ: being a stranger is part of the ministry imposed upon him.

We do not know how Patrick imagined the physical world, but we sense that he thought of Ireland and Britain as far apart. Certainly, the actual place of his captivity as a youth is very far from his home: it is a long journey from the Western Sea to where one can sail home (*Conf.* 17), and then there is the barrier of the sea (*Conf.* 18). But if he thinks of these islands as far apart, Britain and Gaul seem very close (*Conf.* 43). A journey to Britain is a major step and one he is unwilling to take once he had returned to Ireland, despite its personal benefits. But if he did go to Britain, then a stay in Gaul with those he desires to see would be one of the added benefits which could be had without difficulty.[13] Distances for an individual's travel are as much a matter of imagination as geography: being in Ireland is dwelling far out from the centre and where all the people who matter personally to him live and returning home again at the time when he is writing involves was we could call 'excessive travel costs.' It seems that from Ireland to anywhere in the Roman world is a major journey over obstacles and frontiers; but any journey within the empire is just popping into the neighbours. Britain and Gaul are imaged as very close together;

---

[13] In a diagram in *Celtic Theology*, p. 38, I have attempted a re-construction of how the various geographical locations mentioned by Patrick may have been related, one to another, by him.

Britain and Ireland are very far apart.

III   An Old Man

In view of the quantity of ink used on the question of Patrick's dates of arrival, death, and age at death in the last century any comment on the topic is a fraught matter. The question is how did Patrick view the Irish episodes within the events of his life. That the two periods in Ireland, first as a slave to a man, then as a slave to the gospel, form the pillars structuring his life's story as presented in the *Confessio* there is no doubt. However, how they relate to one another within his personal sense of time is another matter.

The first period begins in youth, about sixteen, and is presented as having all the folly of youth in attendance (*Conf.* 1, 2, 9, 10, 12). Patrick gives us a little information about the length of this first Irish episode: "Shortly after that I took to flight, left the man with whom I had been for six years, and journeyed ..." (*Conf.* 17). However, we should note that when we take this as referring to the whole period of his time as a captive,[14] it assumes that he had only one master. But it is most probably the whole length of his stay for this would accord with the way he introduces the Victoricus visitation: "Again after few years I was in Britain with my parents"[15] (*Conf.* 23). He presents it as a period of learning and growing to know "the true God" (*Conf.* 1 and 44 provide examples), so that when he travelled home he was one who prayed and was aware of the workings of the Spirit within him. The early years were ones of probation and initiation: that he could then leave Ireland is equivalent to a graduation.

Matters become more complicated when it comes to his second trip to Ireland. The sequence of events as noted in the *Confessio* presents his call to go back to Ireland as taking place very soon after his return from slavery (*Conf.* 23), and we imagine that this trip to Ireland was not too long after that again. However, he assumes that we know that there was a very long period – at least several decades – between the two Irish episodes. The evidence can be set out like this. The *Confessio* appears to be written in what he considered to be his old age, though we cannot quantify what he considered 'old age' to mean. In *Confessio* 10 he contrasts the time of his writing with that of his youth and describes it as "in my old age" (*in*

---

[14] E.g. P. Salway, *Roman Britain* (Oxford, 1981), p. 462.

[15] *Et iterum post paucos annos in Brittanniis eram cum parentibus meis, ...*

senectute mea); and this coheres with his statement at the end of the work (*Conf.* 62) that he writes it before he dies. But this second Irish episode is presented as having begun in what he considered to be his advanced years: "On the other hand, I was not setting out for Ireland until I was approaching my declining years" (*donec prope deficiebam*) (*Conf.* 28). Similarly, in an earlier place he noted it was "after many years had gone by" that his mission began (*Conf.* 5).[16] And this sense of many years fits with what he says about the sin confessed before he became a deacon, and thirty years (*post annos triginta*) before any accusation was made against him (*Conf.* 27).[17] Granted he was sixteen when taken captive, and spent at least six years in Ireland, then the earliest he could have been ordained deacon is twenty-two.[18] So the earliest age at which an accusation could be made is fifty-two, and he wrote sometime after that. In fact, we could add some years on to this, and assume that in 'the declining years' (when he set out for Ireland as a missionary) refers possibly to his forties or fifties.

However we might construe his incidental remarks, one point seems clear: his life has two significant periods, one in youth, the other in mature age, both in Ireland. From his perspective at the time of writing the *Confessio* the rest of his life, even though it seems to be longer in quantity of time, is less real, no more than the duration separating the times in Ireland. His real life is in these two periods. It appears as if he saw himself as a part of the structure of a greater history (the history in which the Word is made known)[19] while he is serving (either a human master in the time of

---

[16] His statement that "after many years he was taken captive again" (*Conf.* 21) does not help us for all this tells us is that there was a long period between his youth and this event.

[17] That there was a lengthy span of time between his two periods in Ireland is corroborated by the fact that there was a major development in Patrick's understanding of his being taken captive aged sixteen: the young Patrick saw it as a punishment and recalls that understanding, but Patrick at the time he wrote the *Confessio* appears to see the matter as an essential preparation located within God's providence (cf. *Celtic Theology*, pp. 31-35).

[18] It is tempting to try to be more precise by examining the 'canonical ages' for ordination to the diaconate. However, this is useless for two reasons: first, and most importantly, since he claims that the sin took place before he was made deacon it had to have been between when he returned from Ireland (at 22) and whatever age he was made deacon, so all we can say is that he was at least 52 when the accusation was made; second, appeals to such documents as the letter of 385 ('*Directa ad decessorem*') of Pope Siricius to Himerius of Tarragona (*P.L.* 67, 236-7) which mention the ages for promotion to the various orders assume that there was a variety of practice in this matter.

[19] This becomes clearer when we look at how he saw a connection between the preaching of the gospel and the eschaton.

probation, a divine master (*Conf.* 49) during his mission) in Ireland. Hence these periods stand out in his own perception of his personal history. And events before Ireland, or between Irish visits are only incidental; they are not important, even if others in criticism might think so.

While Patrick's omission of details about his time outside Ireland might frustrate the historian – or even a hagiographer like Muirchú – it does reveal part of his humanity. For when we recall our own past, without deliberately attempting to recall events in manner of an historian as when, for example, we are compiling a c.v., we notice that some periods and events stand out from the rest of life as its times of significance. The rest of the time can appear as if the person is standing still with time passing behind them as a backdrop. This selection of the important periods of one's life is personal time at its most real.

IV   In the Uttermost Parts
One of the phrases that recurs in Patrick is that he is in "the uttermost part of the earth" (*Conf.* 1, 34, 38; *Ep.* 9) or similar expressions. These phrases, which for Patrick locate the position of Ireland, are taken from the New Testament. In Lk 11:31 (= Mt 12:42) Christ tells of the 'Queen of the South' who came from the ends of the earth (*a finibus terrae*) to hear Solomon's wisdom. In *Acts* 1:8 and 13:47, both of which are in Patrick's mind at the opening of the *Confessio*,[20] "the ends of the earth" are linked to the preaching of the gospel: the Spirit will make the apostles witnesses to Christ in Jerusalem, the surrounding areas, and right out to the end of the earth (Acts 1:8: *usque ad ultimum terrae*) and thus the apostles are set up as light for the salvation of the nations out to the very end of earth (*Acts*

---

[20] The text of *Confessio* 1 reads: ... *et Dominus 'induxit super' nos 'iram'* [Is 42:25] *'animationis suae et dispersit nos in gentibus'* [the concept of dispersal among the nations as a divine punishment for infidelity is found in many places in the Old Testament, but especially in the prophets where it is presented as just reward of the people: Lev 26:33 and 38; Deut 4:27; Ps 106:27; 1 Chr 16:35; Jer 9:16; Lam 1:3 and 2:9; Hos 9:17; Zech 10:9; Ezek 4:13, 5:14, 6:8, 11:16, 12:15-6, 20:23, 22:15, 25:10, 29:12, 30:23 and 26, 32:9, 36:19, and 39:28; and it is found in Joel 2:19 and 3:2 – a prophet is echoed in the next section – and in Tob 13:4-7 which seems to be reflected in several ways by Patrick in this section] *multis etiam 'usque ad ultimum terrae'* [this final phrase is taken from *Acts* 1:8: *sed accipietis uirtutem superuenientis Spiritus Sancti in uos et eritis mihi testes in Hierusalem et in omni Iudaea et Samaria et usque ad ultimum terrae*; however, it follows on *gentibus* and so picks up the memory of Acts 13:47: *sic enim praecepit nobis Dominus posui te in lumen gentibus ut sis in salutem usque ad extremum terrae*].

13:47: *usque ad extremum terrae*). Moreover, the notion that the gospel is heard at the ends of the earth (*in fines orbis terrae*) is also found, but with a different focus, in Rm 10:18 which quotes Ps 18:4: "their voice [the heavens' proclamation] goes out through all the earth, and their words to the ends of the world." So Scripture provides a framework to locate where Patrick finds himself located by the will of God. He has been sent to the last place among all the lands, to the furthest out nation, first by a divine judgement and latterly by a divine commission.

In Lk/Acts we have the story of the early preaching which presents the message of Jesus spreading through Jerusalem (preaching to Jews); next, through the apostles, to the surrounding areas (also Jews); and then, through the journeys of Paul, reaching 'the nations' (Gentiles) within the Roman Empire. Luke makes clear that this is a three stage process.[21] This can be represented as a message spreading through three concentric circles. But as Patrick sees it, the limit of the preaching up to his time was the boundary of the Empire in the west, but there were a few places even beyond that. Now he has gone out there to the very end, to the nations that are beyond the reach of everyone until then. He is with the nation that is in the furthest west (*Conf.* 39) to carry out this commission to teach the nations[22] (*Conf.* 40 and *Ep.* 1). Indeed, he has gone beyond where people live (*Conf.* 51), right out to the shore of the western sea (*Conf.* 23).

The probability is that Patrick thought out the world to be something like this.[23] Towards the centre of the great land mass of the earth was the city of Jerusalem, and around it the promised land. Around this were ranged the nations (cf. Ezek 5:5), and their lands stretched out to the Ocean. Most of this land-mass was held by the Romans, but out on the fringe was, at least, one place outside both the orbit of Rome and Jerusalem: Ireland. It was in the land of the west; and its location destined it to be the outer limit of preaching, and thus one extreme of the *catholica* for from there to the

---

[21] Lk 24:47 and Acts 1:8; and note that same theme can be found in Acts 2:14-32.

[22] Cf. Mt 28:19; which is quoted in the *Confessio* and alluded to in the *Epistola*.

[23] This is explicitly how Isidore of Seville (d. 630) viewed the world. However, while Isidore is very different to Patrick – not just in time, but as a bookworm who loved to create synthetic overviews of topics – he drew on the same biblical notions for his basic vision, and on the same general Christian ideas about the action of the body of Christ in the world that Patrick is drawing upon. On the background to Isidore on this question, cf. my 'The View from Iona: Adomnán's Mental Maps,' loc. cit., and my 'Living in the Ocean' in C. Bourke ed., *Studies in the Cult of Saint Columba* (Dublin, 1987), pp. 11-23.

furthest east people were summoned to Lord's banquet.[24] That Patrick is thinking in this structural way about his location is confirmed, possibly, by his addition[25] of the other two 'corners'[26] of the earth, north and south, to his citation of Mt 8:11: "I tell you, many will come from east and west, *and south and north*, and sit at table with Abraham, Isaac, and Jacob in the kingdom of heaven" (*Conf.* 39). And the particular people being called, through him, to the banquet is from the extremity of earth (*ab extremis terrae*) (*Conf.* 38).[27] Patrick is someone operating out on the final frontier. He appears to have imagined his location thus: (*see opposite page*)

Through his work the message of the gospel, which originated at the centre and had been carried to the nearby nations by the first apostles as recorded in *Acts*, was brought out to the very last piece of land (*ad ultimum terrae*).

V   On the Edge of the Eschaton
If Patrick imagines his location as being on the edge, the borders, the last place, of the lands; he has a similar view of his place in history: he belongs to the last times, and the end is imminent. Indeed, the end will not be

---

[24] The notion that the eschatological Eucharist, the perfect offering, will involve people from the extremes of the earth, from the east to the west, and that this will constitute the whole of the Church is common among the Fathers, yet I know of no monograph that explores it in detail: the following texts are central to the image: Ps 106:3; Is 49:12; 59:19; Mal 1:11; and Mt 8:11; and note that it is developed in the Eucharistic Prayer texts in the Didache 9 and 10.

[25] The addition is not found in the Bieler edition, but is in the text of N.J.D. White: *sicut in euangelio pollicetur: Uenient ab oriente et occidente et ab austro et ab aquilone, et recumbent cum Abraham et Isaac et Iacob; sicut credimus ...* . Here White follows the text of the Book of Armagh (fol. 24ʳ) which, here, is the text to be preferred as this addition is not just the result of a scribe 'filling out' a quotation from memory; first in that the phrase 'from east to west' (or variants of it such as 'from the rising of the sun to its setting') are common in scripture while 'from north to south' or from all four points are not; and second, in the text of Mt in the Book of Armagh (fol. 37ʳᵃ) this addition is not found – if this addition were a peculiarity of the scribe's gospel text it should have affected the gospel itself as much as the text of the *Confessio*.

[26] The notion of the earth having four corners is found in Is 11:12; 41:9; Apoc 7:1; and 20:8.

[27] He presents this as the fulfilment of a prophesy in Jer 16:19; and then returns to the Lukan theme of the gospel spreading from Jerusalem by quoting Acts 13:47.

54

THE EAST
(Mt 8:11; *Conf.* 39)

THE NORTH
(Mt 8:11; *Conf.* 39)

Jerusalem
(Acts 1:8)

Israel : Judea and Samaria
(Mt 10:23) (Acts 1:8)

THE SOUTH
(Mt 8:11; *Conf.* 39)

The lands of the 'Holy Romans' (*Ep.* 2; 14)
where the first apostles preached

Gaul (*Conf.* 43)
Britain (*Conf.* 43)

Ireland
final nation (Acts 1:8; 13:47; Mt 24:14; *Conf.* 1; 34; 38)
last inhabited place (*Conf.* 34; 51)
where Patrick preaches (Mt 28:19; *Conf.* 40)

The Western Sea
[The Ocean] (*Conf.* 23)

THE WEST
(Mt 8:11; *Conf.* 39)

PATRICK'S WORLD ?

delayed very long after the completion of his own work in Ireland. He develops this theme in the central section of the *Confessio* by seeing a direct relationship between the preaching of the gospel and the close of human history.

The theme is announced by Patrick thanking God for the task he has been given in "the last days" (*in nouissimis diebus*). The basis for his belief that he lives in the final times is that God has promised that he would "announce his gospel before all nations before the world's end." Now, Patrick is the instrument of this proclamation, and with his fellow Irish Christians, he bears witness to it at the very limits of the inhabited world (*ubi nemo ultra est*) (*Conf.* 34). So we presume that since everywhere has now heard the gospel, there is nothing to delay the end, so it is now close at hand! This reasoning becomes clearer when he re-states his position a little further on.

Having announced repeatedly that he has preached the gospel at the ends of the earth, and how thus a prophesy is fulfilled, (*Conf.* 37-39); Patrick turns to the basis of all his work: Christ' command to preach (*Conf.* 40). He strings together three roughly parallel[28] texts: first, Mt 28:19-20:

> Go therefore and make disciples of all nations, baptising them in the name of the Father and of the Son and of the Holy Spirit, teaching them to observe all that I have commanded you; and behold, I am with you all days until the consummation,

---

[28] Most synopses (e.g. A. Huck - H. Greeven, *Synopse der drei ersten Evangelien* (13e, Tübingen, 1981), or B.H. Throckmorton, *Gospel Parallels: A Synopsis of the First Three Gospels* (New York, 1949)) do not present any of these verses in parallel as they are not verbally alike; however, this should not obscure the fact that they do share a common structure and context within the synoptic tradition. Mt 24:14 and 28:19-20 can be seen as a couplet: the command to preach is announced, and then repeated at the decisive moment at the end of the gospel. Mk 16: 15-6 belongs to the longer ending that was added to Mk and which is based on Mt: in this case the context is supplied by Mt 28:19-20 but the language echoes Mt 24:14. The command to preach in Lk (24:47 to which we have already referred) is linguistically distinct from Mt, but falls in the same position within his text as Mt 28:19-20 in its text. We can therefore conclude that a command to preach (in some form) was part of the double tradition and was handled differently according to each writer's theological perspective (eschatological in the case of Mt; the message spreading to the ends of the earth in the case of Lk); and, Mk is derived from the Matthaean form. While Patrick sees the links between these verses through a very different optic, the actual combination is a sound one.

second, Mk 16: 15-6

> Go, therefore, into all the world and preach the gospel to every creature; whoever believes and is baptised will be saved; but whoever does not believe will be condemned,

and finally Mt 24:14

> This gospel of the kingdom will be preached throughout the whole world, as a testimony to all nations; and then will come the end.

As Patrick reads these verses they convey a single structure: preaching followed by completion, preaching followed by judgement, preaching followed by the end. For him, the second event – the final judgement that marks the end of the age – is the direct consequence of the completion of the task of preaching. Put simply, once everyone has heard the gospel then there will be no further reason to delay the End. Patrick sees this as a plan in the divine mind for the period between the Ascension and the return of Christ in the Last Times (see *Conf.* 35). Moreover, this vast plan for the history of the world is something that addresses and involves him in a particular way. He is the one who is preaching in the very last place on earth to the very last nation to hear the message. As such Patrick sees himself as the final preacher in a chain going back to the apostles. He has had a unique task given to him, for when he has finished his work in Ireland, then the preaching phrase of history is finished. With history complete, the universe enters the next stage in God's plan: the End. And in the very next sentence (*Conf.* 41) Patrick announces the state of history: the gospel has reached Ireland, the outermost place, and those who had only known idols are now "the prepared people" (Lk. 1:17) of the Lord and the children of God.[29] Although Patrick never quotes the verse he seems to have Mt 10:23 ("When they persecute you in one town, flee to the next; for truly, I say to you, you will not have gone through all the towns of Israel, before the Son of man comes"), or something like it, in mind in formulating his theory. There is a fixed quantum of time before the End,

---

[29] Here I follow White's edition (*quomodo nuper perfecta est plebs Domini et filii Dei nuncupantur*); while this appears to be the *lectio difficilior*, by echoing Lk it makes the purpose of the whole sentence clear.

this is determined by the need to preach everywhere, and it is not as great as the length of time needed to get around all the towns of Israel. In any case, there is no need for more time as the given task is completed.

When we reflect on Patrick's humility[30] we should remember that he presents himself as having a singular place in bringing about the consummation of creation. And, with this knowledge we are in a better position for understanding the urgency he must have felt when he referred to living in "the last days" (*Conf.* 34; and *Ep.* 10). This may also throw light on his expansion of credal statement, "who is to come again" (*et iterum uenturus est*), to the more pointed: "and whose coming we look for soon" (*expectamus aduentum ipsius mox futurum*) (*Conf.* 4).

VI Conclusion

Constructing mental maps from literary remains is a process of interpretation that yields results with a low index of certainty. This fact alone raises questions as to the utility of the endeavour. Yet such pictures of one's place in space and time are part of our human consciousness; hence, at the very least, asking these questions – whether they can be answered to any appreciable extent – is justified. In Patrick's case we can be certain of this much: he saw himself as a stranger in Ireland working on the fringes of human space and time. His work of evangelisation belongs to the final, and most difficult, phase of a process that began with the sending out of the apostles by Christ to the whole world (Mt), starting with Jerusalem and reaching out to every nation out to the very ends of the earth (Lk /Acts). He, Patrick, has carried out successfully his part in this work, so his finishing his work coincides with the completion of the whole apostolic task. The completion of this task ushers in the completion, the judgement, the coming of the Son of Man in glory. So the return of the Christ at the end, foretold in the scriptures and confessed in the creed, cannot be far, in external time, in the future.

I wish to express my gratitude to the Pantyfedwen Fund of the University of Wales Lampeter for a grant which enabled me to carry out some of the research for this paper.

---

[30] *Conf.* 1 and 55 for example.

RECURRING THEMES IN CATULLUS AND VIRGIL.
Catullus: Poems 63, 64, 68; Virgil: *Aeneid* IV, *Georgics* IV.

John O'Meara

My long and friendly collaboration with the Professors of Greek and Latin in Maynooth (1947-1984) may allow me the indulgence of recalling, with pleasure and esteem, the names of Denis Meehan and William Meany, while I contribute more formally to this *Festschrift* in honour of Gerard Watson and Thomas Finan. Here I have essayed a topic to which, I feel, Thomas Finan, fine and sensitive scholar that he is, would have done greater credit.

On the face of it the passages to be reviewed deal with love stories. It is clear, however, that they are something more. All concentrate on love confronted by the possibility of the irrevocable total loss of the loved one. It is my hope that in examining closely these stories and their contrasts we may gain some light on the nature of Catullus' love for Lesbia on the one hand, and the suitability of the Orpheus – Eurydice episode as an ending to the *Georgics* on the other.

I am taking it as accepted that Virgil, who would have been sixteen years of age in 54 B.C. when Catullus may have died, who came from Mantua (so close to Catullus' birth-place, Verona), and whose work shows undeniable acquaintance with Catullus' work, is likely to have known Catullus' versions of the Laudamia – Protesilaos and Ariadne – Theseus stories. The question arises if Catullus' vignettes affected Virgil's version of Orpheus and Eurydice and if so, how? Do they help, for example, in clarifying the significance of the Orpheus – Eurydice episode?

It has been suggested in 1969 by L.P. Wilkinson[1], for example, that Catullus' treatment of Ariadne and Theseus within the wider story of Peleus and Thetis in poem 64 is a crucial exemplar in relation to the Orpheus – Eurydice episode and that Virgil's handling of this episode within the wider Aristaeus 'epyllion' was 'in the spirit of Catullus'. Otis[2] had already in 1963 drawn attention to this likelihood. Finally Klingner in the same year

---

[1] L.P. Wilkinson, *The Georgics: A Critical Survey* (Cambridge, 1969), pp. 115-16.
[2] B. Otis, *Virgil: A Study in Civilized Poetry* (Oxford, 1963), p. 193.

had drawn attention to Catullus' version of the Laudamia – Protesilaos story. In all cases the episodes in question are placed within wider frames which provide strong contrasting themes. Our enquiry, therefore, is not novel. It will, however, concern itself with the texts[3] involved themselves, not with the secondary literature

If I start with poem 68 of Catullus, containing the story of Laudamia and Protesilaos, I do not imply that it can be placed chronologically before poem 64 of Catullus. It does appear, however, to allude to an early period of Catullus' *affaire* with Lesbia:

> isque domum nobis isque dedit dominae...
>   quo mea se molli candida diua pede
> intulit...
>   coniugis ut quondam flagrans aduenit amore
>   Protesilaeam Laudamia domum (68.68ff.)

It is to be noted that Catullus here explicitly compares Lesbia to Laudamia but, hardly without significance, only on the point of their both arriving at a house, a *domus*, the house of their loved one. This implies that Lesbia, like Laudamia, was interested in the meeting, that is, with Catullus. But Catullus speaks here rather of Lesbia's god-like beauty than of any passion that she had for him. Later in the poem he freely admits her infidelities and is grateful if she does not treat him casually:

> quare illud satis est, si nobis is datur unis
>   quem lapide illa dies candidiore notat. (147 ff.)

Laudamia, on the other hand, is immediately portrayed as *flagrans amore* and that extravagance of passion is insisted upon throughout the poem. However, there can be little doubt but that, paradoxically, Laudamia's love represents not Lesbia's love, but Catullus' own. He takes pride elsewhere in asserting that Lesbia was loved by him more than any woman ever:

> nulla potest mulier tantum se dicere amatam
>   uere, quantum a me Lesbia amata mea est. (87.1-2.)

---

[3] All texts used are from the Scriptorum Classicorum Bibliotheca Oxoniensis.

....
puella nam mi, quae meo sinu fugit,
amata tantum quantum amabitur nulla. (37. 11-12)

....
illa Lesbia, quam Catullus unam
plus quam se atque suos amauit omnes. (58. 2-3)

Scholars have suggested that Ariadne, for example, *vis-à-vis* Theseus, represents Catullus *vis-à-vis* Lesbia. I take this to be so. In so far as Attis in poem 63 reveals to a significant extent the same situation and language used by Ariadne, I feel that Attis, that is Attis become female, represents Catullus also – a context, however, not of love, but of attempted sublimation of love. This suggests too that Laudamia in poem 68 stands in for Catullus. The repeated use of *domus* in 68.68-74 to bring Lesbia and Laudamia together and so discuss their loving is, I believe, of no small significance for the understanding of Catullus. *Domus*, as indeed Witke has already, suggested, is a symbol of love. This is not an unimportant point to which I shall return presently.

For the moment we should return to the Laudamia episode itself. Catullus does not so much tell us the story as elaborate upon the depth of Laudamia's passion. But it is essential to bear in mind that Protesilaus, her love, was killed at Troy and, since he was said to be the very first to be killed there, may possibly be used as a symbol of death in Troy. Catullus alludes to this in the phrase *amisso uiro* which, in the context, might well not suggest to the reader any more than that he was lost to her embraces. Nevertheless Catullus removes any doubt but that Laudamia was destined to be a widow:

> posset ut abrupto uiuere coniugio,
> quod scibant Parcae non longo tempore abesse,
> si miles muros isset ad Iliacos. (84 ff.)

And he clearly alludes to burial:

> Troia (nefas!) commune sepulcrum Asiae Europaeque,
> Troia uirum et uirtutum omnium acerba cinis,
> quaene etiam nostro letum miserabile fratri
> attulit. (89 ff.)

61

Troy here, then, may symbolize the death of love and death itself: *commune sepulcrum*. What may seem astonishing, however, is that Catullus reports, without transition, that Troy brought about, not only the death of the Argives but also that of his brother (93 ff.). Such sudden conjuncture of fiction and 'fact' is, indeed, not uncommon in contemporary Latin, including Virgilian, literature. It is also true that there is some evidence, including a repetition of this passage referring to his brother's death both within this poem 68 (20 ff., assuming that it is one poem) and elsewhere (101.6 ff., 77.4), to suggest that the poem is unfinished and that, perhaps, Catullus introduced these lines about his brother's death here only provisionally. Nevertheless we should, perhaps, be prepared to take account of another possible explanation of the reference to this brother's death at this point.

Whether or not Catullus had a real brother who died at Troy (a matter on which doubt has been cast) the brother here represents another Protesilaos, a man loved by Catullus, as Protesilaos was by Laudamia. Catullus' love is confronted with his loss:

> ei misero frater adempte mihi,
> ei misero fratri iucundum lumen ademptum,
> tecum una tota est nostra sepulta domus. (92 ff.)

One should note most carefully this last line: *domus* cannot, of course, mean a physical house, for to speak of burying physically a physical house here is out of the question. Once again *domus* means love and *sepulta domus* means a love that has suffered death. Despite the sequence of transitions, Laudamia – Troy – death of brother – Troy – Laudamia – the theme remains the same, that is Laudamia's love or, since this appears to be symbolical, Catullus' love of Lesbia. That love is as extravagant as Laudamia's: an extravagance clearly indicated by Ovid:

> Si comes extincti Manes sequerere mariti,
> Esset dux facti Laudamia tui. (*P.* 3. 1.110 ff.)

Laudamia followed her husband to Hades. Catullus' poem does not, scholars think, allude to this. There is, perhaps, nevertheless a curiously indirect and, it may be, unconscious reference to it. Instead of saying that

Laudamia's love confronted Hades, Catullus compares her love to deep underground channels of water:

> ... tanto te absorbens uertice amoris
> aestus in abruptum detulerat barathrum,
> quale ferunt Grai Pheneum prope Cylleneum
> siccare emulsa pingue palude solum. (68.107 ff.)

If these lines suggest that in Catullus' conscious or unconscious mind there lurked the story of Laudamia's following Protesilaos to Hades, or perhaps even that version of the story to which Propertius referred later, namely that Protesilaos was allowed to return briefly to his lamenting wife:

> illic Phylacides iucundae coniugis heros
> non potuit caecis immemor esse locis.
> sed cupidus falsis attingere gaudia palmis
> Thessalus antiquam uenerat umbra domum.
> (E. 1.19.7 ff.)

then we are brought close to Virgil's story, with the sex roles (characteristically as we shall suggest) reversed, of Orpheus and Eurydice. That Virgil knew this poem of Catullus and specifically the lines referring to the deep underground channels can perhaps be inferred from *Aeneid* III:

> atque imo barathri ter gurgite uastos
> sorbet in abruptum fluctus...(421 ff.)

But there was one good reason why Catullus did not in the poem pursue his love to Hades: Lesbia, whatever about a brother, was very much alive.

•　　•　　•　　•　　•

We might now turn to the Ariadne and Theseus vignette which has received rather more attention in the context of the background to Virgil's Orpheus and Eurydice.

The Ariadne and Theseus episode in a way takes up the story precisely at the point where Catullus had brought the story of Laudamia and Protesilaos – the encounter of the latter with the danger of death. In it Theseus descends into the labyrinth and holding to a thread held by Ariadne is brought up safely once again. That the Minotaur in the labyrinth meant death, there can be do doubt:

dapem dare Minotauro. (64.79)

Catullus, however, quite characteristically dwells not so much on the main exploit as on describing the intense passion of Ariadne for Theseus before he entered the labyrinth and her equally intense but destructive passion for him after he had deserted her. As in the case of Laudamia, Catullus' preoccupation is the passion of love as it variously expresses itself, positively or negatively, and the passion is his alone. But the emotion centrally and most powerfully presented is a love turned hate because of abandonment. It was a traditional theme, the prototype of which is the story of Medea.

The essential elements in this experience – described also by Virgil in *Aeneid* IV – are uncontrolled passion, a rude awakening, remorse and an effort to wreak vengeance on a false lover. Catullus' portrayal of such uncontrolled passion, rude awakening and remorse is the dominant feature of the Ariadne episode.

To digress briefly – this theme is also most significantly paralleled in the Attis poem (63). There the key-word is *furor* (54, 94, 124, 197), followed closely by *rabies* and *uagus*. All suggest irrational frenzy. Then comes with sleep and the cold light of dawn the stark realization of a clear mind, *liquida mente*. There follows remorse, poignant regret for what has been surrendered in a passion that is now recognized as wrong. A reading of the Attis poem and the Ariadne episode reveals an extraordinary concentration, repeated even within the Ariadne episode itself, on identical themes and expressions. It can only mark the extreme pre-occupation of Catullus with these themes.

The Attis poem, I believe, in the context in which I have now put it, may be very revealing of the character of Catullus. The love object here is not consciously Lesbia or any person – which is not to say that she may not, nevertheless, unconsciously in fact be the real object. It is ostensibly Cybele. The poem treats of the sublimation of human love in the service of a goddess. That sublimation is attended by self-emasculation crudely performed and exposure to a Dionysiac, not to say savage, way of life. But the sublimation quickly fails, and Catullus prays to be spared from such madness:

procul a mea tuos sit furor omnis, era, domo! (92)

This poem suggests that Catullus, for all his love of Lesbia or Juventius or others – or perhaps because of his frustration with them all – felt the attraction of some mystical or perhaps religious ideal but rejected it. This has already been suggested by Granorlo, and it cannot be considered to be impossible. Nevertheless, one can still interpret the poem as in fact referring to his love of Lesbia. In his infatuation with her, mere physical passion had been obliterated. The idea of his love for her threatened to become an *obsession*. If this corresponded to the actuality, then Catullus did well to pray to be delivered from such a love. But does not such a reading of the poem raise the relevant question if Catullus' love for Lesbia was mostly a product of his heated imagination? Whatever reading one takes of this poem Catullus emerges from it as having an introvert side. The tension implied in such a conjuncture is paralleled in the conjuncture of clarity and obscure learning in his poetry. It will not, I hope, have escaped notice that, when Catullus prays that he may escape such a passion as Attis suffered, he uses the term *domus*: *procul a mea domo*. The reference cannot be to his physical home and can only be to *himself*. *Domus* is, then, self-regarding, whether it stands for Catullus himself or his loving, and underlines once again his introvert side.

• • • • •

Ariadne, however, has a real object for her love and her revenge – Theseus. As in the case of Protesilaos we know from his deed that he is brave and we are told that he was *flauus*. In fact, however, Theseus, like Protesilaos, is a silent *persona*, the mere focus of his lover's emotions. Laudamia's emotions were intense and all of love. Ariadne's are also intense but have turned to hate. One crime of Theseus is singled out for emphasis and on it the sequel hinges: his heedlessness. *Immemor* or some such word recurs over and over again in the episode as in the Attis poem (63. 58, 123, 135). Ariadne taxes Theseus with more than simple forgetfulness: it is self-regarding heedlessness; in her rage she suggests that he deceived her intentionally and that his promises were vain – but this too, of course, is a

65

manifestation of pre-occupation with selfish interests. And so when she comes to wreak her vengeance on Theseus she uses this very heedlessness of his:

> sed quali solam Theseus me mente reliquit,
> tali mente, deae, funestet seque suosque. (64.200 ff.)

Theseus' father had bidden him to change from a dark to a white sail if he returned safely, having killed the Minotaur, to Athens.

> facito ut memori tibi condita corde
> haec uigeant mandata, nec ulla oblitteret aetas. (231 ff.)

Great emphasis is put by Catullus on the fact that Theseus did keep his father's bidding *constanti mente* (238). Nevertheless, doubtless because of Jupiter's acceding to Ariadne's request, his mind became obscured and he finally forgot it.

And so Catullus concludes:

> Theseus, qualem Minoidi luctum
> obtulerat mente immemori, talem ipse recepit. (247)

To the episode is appended about fifteen lines dealing with Dionysius and Ariadne which describes in usual terms a Bacchic rout. It bears resemblance with 63, the Attis poem – an indication of how poems 63, 64 and 68 are intertwined, perhaps unfinished.

Before we leave Catullus and Ariadne we might observe how important such terms as *furor* and *immemor* are seen to be. Lack of consciousness in love exposes one to danger, including the danger of what arises from the lack of reciprocation of another. Catullus portrayed himself as being aware of all of this. Lesbia's lack of response left its mark on him: *odi et amo*. One might regard Ariadne and Laudamia as the corresponding symbols of his love. But he could not help himself. He could not carry out his own injunction: *Miser Catulle, desinas ineptire* (8.1). Once again we are led to ask if his love of Lesbia was not to a large extent an *affaire* of his mind?

•　　•　　•　　•　　•

I now turn to the fourth book of Virgil's *Aeneid*. If I take it before the Orpheus and Eurydice episode of *Georgic* IV I do not imply by this that this is the order of their composition. It is quite simply a matter of convenience in this paper.

The resemblance of the Ariadne and Theseus episode of Catullus' poem 64 to the Dido and Aeneas episode in *Aeneid* IV does not need to be demonstrated, and it would be tedious to dwell upon the many parallels of every kind between the two: it is rather like the parallel between Attis and Ariadne in poems 63 and 64 of Catullus – but on a grander scale. And of course there are many literary and rhetorical influences in all of these vignettes, above all the traditional picture of Medea. One might remark simply, in passing, on the recurrence of some form of the term *furor* (91, 101, 283, 298, 433, 465, 474, 501, 548, 646, 670, 697) to describe Dido's passion. Likewise both she and Aeneas are guilty of not remembering their vows and obligations:

> regnorum immemores turpique cupidine captos (194);

> oblitos famae melioris amantis (221);

> heu, regni rerumque oblite tuarum (267).

Aeneas uses the word *memor* in a special way. He asserts that he will remember Dido as long as he remembers himself, as long as he breathes:

> nec me meminisse pigebit Elissae
> dum memor ipse mei, dum spiritus hos regit artus. (345 ff.)

It is difficult to avoid the impression that here, as in the Ariadne and Theseus episode, there is a crucial tension intended between the freneticism of love or love become hate on the one hand, and alert and provident consciousness on the other.

· · · · ·

In *Aeneid* VI we enter not the labyrinth of poem 64 of Catullus but Hades – a Hades from which souls return to earth in transmigration. Aeneas descends to the nether world and there encounters Dido. There is no question of his having gone down to the realm of Pluto to bring her up again. As in *Aeneid* IV he shows himself committed to carrying out his orders to found Italy: his fatherland is his love: *hic amor, haec patria est.* He does, however, want to console her. But she has turned against him, hard as the oak or rock.

•   •   •   •   •

And now we come to the Orpheus and Eurydice episode in Virgil's *Georgics* IV. 315 ff. In Virgil the centre of emotional attention has shifted from the woman to the man – to Orpheus. In Catullus all the emotional intensity centres on Laudamia, on Ariadne, on Attis – all figures, as I think, of Catullus. In the episode of Dido and Aeneas in *Aeneid* IV the preponderance of emotional intensity is also with the woman. But the man, Aeneas, is near the centre of the stage; there is over-all approval of his action, but he too suffers an emotional storm:

> mens immota manet lacrimae uoluuntur inanes (449)

In the case of *Georgics* IV the woman has become the relatively inactive partner and Orpheus it is who does and suffers all, including disaster and death in the end.

The climax of this moving episode comes when Orpheus in the madness of his love forgets the injunction that had been imposed upon him – not to look back on Eurydice:

> cum subita incautum dementia cepit amantem,
> ....
> restitit, Eurydicenque suam iam luce sub ipsa
> immemor heu! uictusque animi respexit. ibi omnis
> effusus labor (488 ff.)

There can be no doubt here but that the word *immemor* marks the crisis of the episode. Orpheus could not be accused by Eurydice, as was Theseus by Ariadne, and Aeneas by Dido, of being treacherous – *perfidus*. She does accuse him of *furor*, the *furor* of love.

> 'quis et me' inquit 'miseram et te perdidit, Orpheu,
> quis tantus furor? (494 ff.)

68

I have looked at passages in Catullus and in Virgil dealing with love. They are found in various structures such as an 'epyllion' or a Dionysiac context or in the context of a descent beneath the earth. The emotional language and rhetorical structures recur in an unmistakable manner. Placed in this context – and I repeat that I am not assuming that the Orpheus and Eurydice episode was written by Virgil *after Aeneid* IV or VI – one wonders if one can come to any more confident conclusions on the important question of the significance of the Aristaeus 'epyllion' placed by Virgil at the end of *Georgics* IV?

I would like to begin by saying that I take it as axiomatic that there is progress upwards through the scales of being in the *Georgics* – from the soil to vegetative life and from that to sensitive or animal life. The fourth book, therefore, in my view must deal with the next scale which is rational or intellectual life. It is to be remarked that man's sensible nature is dealt with, when Virgil is dealing with animals, in *Georgics* III, since man shares his sensible nature with them. In particular everything to do with sensible love is powerfully portrayed there as is indeed also the extraordinary unity between man and his world of animals, plants and nature in general, which Virgil reveals in his every phrase:

> Omne adeo genus in terris hominumque ferarumque
> et genus aequoreum, pecudes pictaeque uolucres,
> in furias ignemque ruunt: amor omnibus idem.
> (*G* 3.242).

Book four of the *Georgics*, then, deals with life above the sensitive. To describe this life characterized by intellect, Virgil uses the bees. The bees are chosen because, according to the natural science of Virgil's day, they did not procreate: they were immune from the movements of the flesh. They, unlike us, could operate without emotion. They were determined, however, by a social commitment which was an admirable exemplar for man in his political organization. The bees shared with all other beings some part of divinity and so were in respect to that part immortal:

> His quidam signis atque haec exempla secuti
> esse apibus partem diuinae mentis et haustus
> aetherios dixere; deum namque ire per omnes

> terrasque tractusque maris caelumque profundum;
> hinc pecudes, armenta, uiros, genus omne ferarum,
> quemque sibi tenuis nascentem arcessere uitas:
> scilicet huc reddi deinde ac resoluta referri
> omnia, nec morti esse locum, sed uiua uolare
> sideris in numerum atque alto succedere caelo. (4.219 ff.)

One should not fail to notice that men are here not listed above animals, but among them. Nor is participation in divinity confined to bees – all beings have it. But bees do exemplify, because of their enforced chastity, the unembarrassed operation of their higher faculty.

We are faced with the question then – are bees according to Virgil in some way superior to men? We can be certain that he had no such idea. We can safely assume in fact that when in the second half of *Georgics* IV he moves from the consideration of bees to the Aristaeus episode he is still moving *upwards* on the scale of being and that, since man is at the centre of that episode, man is supreme and this is in fact the climax of the book.

When Plato found that reason could not formulate the higher truths which he wished to expound, he had recourse to myth – the Cave, the Vision of Er. In *Eclogue* VI Virgil too, having gone as far as he could in giving a very Lucretian and rational explanation of the origin of matter and animals, resorts immediately to myth when he wishes to speak of man.

> Namque canebat uti magnum per inane coacta
> semina terrarumque animaeque marisque fuissent
> et liquidi simul ignis; ut his exordia primis
> omnia et ipse tener mundi concreverit orbis:
> ....
> incipiant siluae cum primum surgere, cumque
> rara per ignaros errent animalia montis
> hinc lapides Pyrrhae iactos, Saturnia regna. (31 ff.)

We can be sure that the transition in *Georgics* IV from bees to Aristaeus and Orpheus is the same transition – from the animal, in which part of a divine faculty was most prominent, upwards to man.

How is man superior to the bees? The answer is in the exercise of responsibility, the exercise of free will: the bees do not appear to exercise the higher functions of intellectual life. And so in the Aristaeus episode you have the vivid contrast between Aristaeus who elected to do what he was told, and Orpheus who failed to do so. The contrast is made the sharper inasmuch as Aristaeus started out by being in the wrong, whereas Orpheus would seem to suffer no such inconvenience. Virgil makes the contrast still sharper by involving our emotions very much with Orpheus and hardly at all with Aristaeus. The lesson is clear: the nobility and depth of human emotion must not come before the recollection of our duty. We should live the life of intellect rather than of sense. Here the terms *memor, immemor* take on their full significance and importance. We should ever keep in mind that we are also intellect. In Virgil's portrayal of man's predicament the greatest threat to this recollection is the *furor*, the *dementia* of human love. In living the life of intellect thus consciously we are, of course, superior to all other animals, including the bees. We are engaged not only in an activity that is worthy of us; we are also forwarding the process of purification whereby all things will be regenerated.

The doctrine vaguely implied here is Platonic and we know with certainty of Virgil's interest in it. It is altogether characteristic of him to convey such doctrine colourfully through myth. And it is altogether proper that the *Georgics* so basically concerned with the world should end on a theme of man's higher destiny. These remarks imply that in my reading of that poem the Aristaeus episode is especially relevant and indeed the necessary climax. One should remark that if lofty doctrine is found here, it is an appropriate place for it. The application of metempsychosis in *Aeneid* VI serves an entirely different purpose: Aeneas is there concerned with founding Rome. It may seem a mere worldly purpose – but it is the one most appropriate to the theme and intention of the *Aeneid*: hence one may not argue that the Aristaeus episode, if loftier, is later.

Virgil in exploiting the Medea – Ariadne theme in both *Georgics* IV and *Aeneid* IV was deliberately employing the intense emotionalism of human love to illustrate at once the difficulty of living up to one's duty, heavenly or earthly, and the inexorable need to do so.

ignoscenda quidem, scirent si ignoscere manes (*G* 4.489)

71

If he echoes the models in Catullus to point up the *furor* of love, it is because these models had been remarkable and probably vivid in his memory. Catullus moreover, for all his absorption with human love, had also shown interest in more serious things, in the labyrinth (a symbol of the after-life) and a mystery cult (a symbol of union with a deity). But he trails behind Virgil not only in profundity, but also, doubtless, in his sensitivity to the theme of love. Both especially contributed to that Italian ('perhaps largely Celtic') genius, which gives (Roman poetry) "its most real title to be called poetry at all."[4]

---

[4] Garrod, W.H., *The Oxford Book of Latin Verse* (Oxford, 1947), pp. xiv, xvii.

A CORRECTION TO *A BRIEF HISTORY OF TIME*

Martin Pulbrook

Professor Stephen Hawking's *A Brief History of Time* has received rave reviews, as well as being a major publishing success. As a classicist, I would not dare to pass comment or judgement on the thesis of the book as a whole. Equally, as a classicist, who taught courses on ancient Greek Science to Maynooth Classics students for fifteen years, I am left aghast at the way that certain Greek scientists are short-changed in Chapter 1 of *A Brief History of Time*. Look at Chapter 1, and look up the Index, and you will see that Pythagoras, Heraclides, Aristarchus and Hipparchus are not mentioned at all. That is an unforgivable omission, particularly as regards Aristarchus. Briefly I shall explain why.

But first a short exposition is in order of the ground actually covered by Hawking in Chapter 1. The two ancient scientists mentioned by Hawking are Aristotle and Ptolemy. Of Aristotle we are told – fairly enough – that "As long ago as 340 BC....Aristotle thought that the earth was stationary and that the sun, the moon, the planets, and the stars moved in circular orbits about the earth."[1] Hawking continues: "This idea was elaborated by Ptolemy in the second century AD into a complete cosmological model. The earth stood at the centre, surrounded by eight spheres that carried the moon, the sun, the stars and the five planets known at the time, Mercury, Venus, Mars, Jupiter and Saturn. The planets themselves moved on smaller circles attached to their respective spheres in order to account for their rather complicated observed paths in the sky. The outermost sphere carried the so-called fixed stars, which always stay in the same positions relative to each other but which rotate together across the sky."

And, having summed up the view of the ancient world as "the Aristotelian/Ptolemaic theory", Hawking explains that this theory remained current up to the century bounded by the years 1514 and 1609: "Ptolemy's model...was adopted by the Christian church as the picture of the universe that was in accordance with Scripture, for it had the great advantage that it left lots of room outside the sphere of fixed stars for heaven and hell. A

---

[1] *A Brief History of Time* (Bantam Books: London, 1995), p. 2. Other passages quoted come from the immediately following pages.

simpler model, however, was proposed in 1514 by a Polish priest, Nicholas Copernicus...His idea was that the sun was stationary at the centre and that the earth and the planets moved in circular orbits around the sun. Nearly a century passed before this idea was taken seriously...the death blow to the Aristotelian/Ptolemaic theory came in 1609. In that year, Galileo started observing the night sky with a telescope, which had just been invented. When he looked at the planet Jupiter, Galileo found that it was accompanied by several small satellites or moons that orbited around it. This implied that everything did *not* have to orbit directly around the earth, as Aristotle and Ptolemy had thought."

From one angle, this is a fair enough summary of the views which were dominant from classical times up to the 16th and 17th centuries. The serious criticism that has to be made of this summary is that it gives no inkling whatsoever that anyone before Copernicus questioned the geocentric theory and suggested an alternative. In fact Heraclides in the mid-4th century – in other words, at or even slightly before the time when Aristotle espoused geocentricity – and Aristarchus a hundred years later did precisely that, and the fact that the prevailing orthodoxy (geocentricity) overwhelmed both of them in their own times, leaving their astronomical work discredited, is no excuse for our forgetting them now, when the thrust of their deductions has, posthumously, been vindicated.

The best modern survey of Heraclides is that of H.B. Gottschalk, published in 1980.[2] And Gerard Watson, reviewing this book in 1981, concluded that "Gottschalk...has done his work well, [and] has given us...certainly a much better and fuller picture of Heraclides than we had."[3] And Watson summarised as follows Gottschalk's view of Heraclides' astronomical studies: "It has sometimes been said that he had arrived at the heliocentric theory, but estimates of his contribution have varied greatly. Gottschalk analyses the evidence carefully and concludes that Heraclides held that the earth rotates about its axis, from west to east, that the sun circles the earth from west to east in a year, and that Mercury and Venus revolve around the sun."

---

[2] *Heraclides of Pontus* (Clarendon Press: Oxford, 1980).
[3] In *Hermathena* CXXX/CXXXI, pp. 121-122.

Heraclides' limited heliocentric theory – limited, that is, to Mercury and Venus – was built on spectacularly by Aristarchus of Samos, who flourished *circa* 280-250 B.C. Archimedes, in his *Arenarius*, quotes a now-lost work by Aristarchus which makes clear that Aristarchus postulated a fully heliocentric theory. In this, Aristarchus anticipated Copernicus. But since Copernicus's work on the heliocentric theory, spanning the thirty years 1513-43 – Copernicus died in 1543 –, predated the *editio princeps* of Archimedes, printed at Basel in 1544, it has been assumed – and most probably the assumption is correct – that Copernicus realised the truth of heliocentricity independently of Aristarchus.[4] That is important, if it is true, but no excuse at all for our remembering Copernicus at Aristarchus's expense.

The loss of the complete writings of Aristarchus is one of the many cultural tragedies consequent upon the destruction, in 48-47 B.C. and A.D. 391 respectively, of the two ancient libraries at Alexandria (The Great Library, founded *c.*300; The Serapeum Library, founded *c.* 250 B.C.). Had these libraries survived, and with them knowledge of Aristarchus's life's work, it is tempting to believe that the heliocentric theory would have returned to centre stage earlier than the time of Copernicus. But the constricting power of tradition and prejudice must never be underestimated. Just as Copernicus's *De revolutionibus orbium coelestim* (1543) was marred, without the dying author's knowledge, by the inclusion of a preface by Andreas Osiander arguing that the thesis of the work was purely hypothetical, and just as Galileo suffered the indignity of a papal decree (1616) that ordered him never again to "defend or hold Copernican astronomical views", so too Aristarchus, for having dared to advance his heliocentric theory, was accused of impiety by the philosopher Cleanthes — for Cleanthes held the Stoic view that the Sun was the dwelling-place of God, the vivifying force of all things, and that, for this reason, the Sun could not possibly be static.

In the absence of Aristarchus's own writings, and in circumstances where we depend on the tangential information provided by Archimedes, it is impossible to make any full-scale assessment of the extent of Aristarchus's

---

[4] Copernicus acknowledged his debt to the Pythagoreans, but not to Aristarchus. It seems reasonable to assume that he would have acknowledged Aristarchus's work, had he known of it.

contribution to heliocentric theory. Clearly he went much further than Heraclides, and it seems a safe assumption that his conclusions came close to those of Copernicus a millennium and three-quarters after him. By any reckoning, his was a phenomenal achievement.

But neither Heraclides nor Aristarchus was applying himself to work on virgin territory, where nobody had toiled before. The casual reader of Chapter 1 of *A Brief History of Time* meets Aristotle's geocentricity of about 340 B.C. as if, in the ancient world, it were the characteristic norm from which no divergence existed. That is grossly misleading, and nothing in fact could be further from the truth. What Hawking gives us is a baldly one-sided picture: it is, frankly, incredible that anyone can write on ancient astronomy without devoting time and space to Pythagoras (born *c*. 582 B.C.).[5] Copernicus himself owed the basis of his heliocentric theory to his exposure as a young man in Italy, during the period 1496-1505, to elements of Pythagoreanism. The significant features of Pythagorean astronomy have been well summed up by Professor A.S. Pringle-Pattison of Edinburgh: "The astronomy of the Pythagoreans was their most notable contribution to scientific thought, and its importance lies in the fact that they were the first to conceive the earth as a globe, self-supported in empty space, revolving with the other planets round a central luminary. They thus anticipated the heliocentric theory. The Pythagoreans did not, however, put the sun in the centre of the system. That place was filled by the central fire to which they gave the names of the hearth of the universe, the watch-tower of Zeus, and other mythological expressions."[6] It is probably fair to see Pythagoras and the Pythagoreans as the primary motivating force both on Heraclides and Aristarchus on the one hand and on Copernicus on the other; without Pythagoras and the Pythagoreans, progress in both subsequent epochs would have been substantially slowed.

None of the foregoing is in any sense new or unknown. As long ago as 1873 G.V. Schiaparelli wrote a short but important article 'I Precursori del Copernico'.[7] These *precursori* merit a mention, however brief, in Hawking's book, rather than to be ignored and passed over.

---

[5] By "Pythagoras" should be understood "Pythagoras and the Pythagoreans"; for to distinguish between the work of the master and that of his followers is no simple task.
[6] In *E.B.*, 13th ed. (1926), XXII, pp. 699-700.
[7] In *Pubbl. del R. Osservatorio di Brera* III, pp. 23-28.

In chapter 1 of *A Brief History of Time*, Hawking, as we have seen, moves straight from Aristotle to Ptolemy in his description of exponents of the geocentric theory. But, even within the limited field of geocentricity, the leaving out of the second-century B.C. astronomer Hipparchus is impossible to defend. The astronomical historian Agnes Mary Clerke has summed up as well as anyone the supreme importance of Hipparchus: "Among the astronomers of antiquity, two great men stand out with unchallenged pre-eminence. Hipparchus and Ptolemy entertained the same large organic designs; they worked on similar methods; and, as the outcome, their performances fitted so accurately together that between them they re-made celestial science. Hipparchus fixed the chief data of astronomy with approximate accuracy. His supreme merit, however, consisted in the establishment of astronomy on a sound geometrical basis. His acquaintance with trigonometry, a branch of science initiated by him, together with his invention of the planisphere, enabled him to solve a number of elementary problems...The choice made by Hipparchus of the geocentric theory of the universe decided the future of Greek astronomy."[8]

All in all, these various points involving unmentioned Greek scientists add up to a substantial criticism of a part, a small part, of *A Brief History of Time*. But I re-emphasize what I wrote at the beginning: I neither wish, nor feel able, to offer constructive criticism of the rest of Hawking's book. At present that book is like a challenging opera introduced, regrettably, by a flawed overture. For the sake of the rest of the opera, the overture needs to be rewritten.

---

[8] In *E.B.*, 13th ed. (1926), II, p. 810.

ARISTOTLE, *POETICS* 1456ª25-32[1]

Keith Sidwell

καὶ τὸν χορὸν δὲ ἕνα δεῖ ὑπολαμβάνειν τῶν ὑποκριτῶν, καὶ μόριον εἶναι τοῦ ὅλου καὶ συναγωνίζεσθαι μὴ ὥσπερ Εὐριπίδῃ ἀλλ᾽ ὥσπερ Σοφοκλεῖ. τοῖς δὲ λοιποῖς τὰ ἀδόμενα οὐδὲν μᾶλλον τοῦ μύθου ἢ ἄλλης τραγῳδίας ἐστίν· διὸ ἐμβόλιμα ἄδουσιν πρώτου ἄρξαντος Ἀγάθωνος τοῦ τοιούτου. καίτοι τί διαφέρει ἢ ἐμβόλιμα ἄδειν ἢ εἰ ῥῆσιν ἐξ ἄλλου εἰς ἄλλο ἁρμόττοι ἢ ἐπεισόδιον ὅλον;

One should consider the chorus too as one of the actors, a part of the whole which helps the poet in the contest, not as in Euripides, but as in Sophocles. As to the rest of them, the choral parts are no more germane to their plots than to some other tragedy. Hence they sing 'inserted lyrics' (Agathon's invention). Yet what is the difference between singing inserted lyrics and putting a speech or a whole episode from one play into another?

The issue I want to raise here concerns not the role of the chorus,[2] but the meaning of Aristotle's expostulation against ἐμβόλιμα "inserted lyrics". Commentators have little or nothing to say about the sentence καίτοι...ὅλον; ("Yet what is the difference...another?").[3] Gudeman, however, claiming the support of the Arabic translation, athetises ἢ ἐπεισόδιον ὅλον, and alters ἁρμόττοι to ἁρμόττειν on the grounds that the usual construction after διαφέρειν in Aristotle is infinitive (there is only one example of εἰ and only

---

[1] I choose to offer our honorands an *exposition* of this passage for a number of reasons. First, Tom Finan was responsible for many years for lecturing on ancient literary criticism at Maynooth, and the text itself can be located in another area for which he had responsibility, Greek tragedy. Gerry Watson, too, sometimes taught tragedy, and his long-standing interest in Aristotle is well known from his scholarly output.

[2] For this, see most recently, Stephen Halliwell, *The Poetics of Aristotle: translation and commentary* (London, 1987), pp. 152-4.

[3] Butcher (1885), Rostagni (1934) say nothing. Lucas (Oxford, 1968) is silent, except for a comment on the probable meaning of ἐπεισόδιον. Else (Michigan, 1967) has nothing to say, and Halliwell (London, 1987) likewise.

one example of a question following διαφέρειν in Aristotle). He asserts that the word-order would have been ῥῆσιν….ἐπεισόδιον ὅλον ἁρμόττειν had the sentence been genuine, and that the addendum spoils the climax of ῥῆσιν…ἁρμόττειν. For him it follows that the addendum was made by a later scholiast familiar with the Roman practice of *contaminatio* in comedy. He gives, however, no real evidence for the phenomenon in respect of tragedy.[4]

Gudeman's reading of the text assumes that later events have overtaken Aristotle's fanciful analogy. The Greek could certainly bear this interpretation, even without the excision. The argument would run something like this:

> The idea of sticking a speech from one play into another is patently absurd. No one would do it. Still less would they put a whole episode from one play into another. Why, then, do we think it reasonable to allow the insertion of lyrics which have no relevance to the plot to be accepted?

This interpretation could be supported by the mood of the verb ἁρμόττοι, taken as a hypothesis.

However, as Gentili remarks:

> Aristotle's contention, notwithstanding the hypothetical form of his approach, does not have the appearance of a theoretical proposition, pure and simple, but very probably reflected what might be called a contaminatory method of compiling dramatic anthologies.[5]

In a note rejecting Gallavotti's assertion that there is no reference here "to the technique of *contaminatio*, brought into use by the Latin comic authors",

---

[4] Alfred Gudeman, *Aristoteles Περὶ Ποιητικῆς* (Berlin, 1934), p. 329: "Was die Tragödie anbelangt, die hier allein in Betracht kommt, so mögen ähnliche Fälle, wie die von A. postulierten, in hellenistischer Zeit mehrfach vorgekommen sein." He follows this with a reference to Vitruvius VII, preface, an anecdote about Aristophanes of Byzantium.

[5] Bruno Gentili, *Theatrical Performances in the Ancient World: Hellenistic and Early Roman Theatre* (Amsterdam/Uithoorn, 1979), p. 21.

Gentili expostulates that:

> ...to anyone interpreting [Aristotle's statement] outside the cultural context in which Aristotle worked, the statement might even seem to be a fictitious hypothesis, in any case extraneous to the mode of argument proper to the *Poetics*, a work which by contrast is always concrete, precise and close to the objective reality of dramatic art.[6]

Gentili may well be correct. However, although he does demonstrate that anthologising was known at this period, what Aristotle mentions here does not suit that process. If concrete, it must relate rather to another phenomenon for which we have some evidence, the alteration of old plays. Let us examine this as the possible cultural context for our passage.

Aristotle is writing in the 330s. And it is precisely to this period that the decree of Lycurgus concerning the text of the three great tragedians belongs. Here is what Plutarch tells us (*Lycurgus* 841F):

> τὸν δέ, ὡς χαλκᾶς εἰκόνας ἀναθεῖναι τῶν ποιητῶν, Αἰσχύλου Σοφοκλέους Εὐριπίδου, καὶ τὰς τραγῳδίας αὐτῶν ἐν κοινῷ γραψαμένους φυλάττειν καὶ τὸν τῆς πόλεως γραμματέα παραναγινώσκειν τοῖς ὑποκρινουμένοις· οὐκ ἐξεῖναι γὰρ παρ' αὐτὰς ὑποκρίνεσθαι.

> [He also introduced] the law that the Athenians should erect bronze statues of the poets Aeschylus, Sophocles and Euripides, write out their tragedies and keep them in a public archive, and that the clerk of the city should read them to those intending to act the plays for comparison, since it was against the law for them to act a different version.

The implications of this decree have been long debated. At one end of the spectrum is the view of Page.[7] According to this, the texts we have of the works of the three great tragedians are peppered with actors' interpolations,

---

[6] *Loc. cit.* previous note, footnote p. 24.

[7] D.L. Page, *Actors' Interpolations in Greek Tragedy* (Oxford, 1934).

which can be identified by their crassness or inappropriateness. At the other end is the view of Hamilton.[8] His feeling is that scholia which ascribe changes in the texts to actors' interpolations are following a theory first thought of in around the first century BC. For Hamilton the law assumes a clean copy of the plays and we should accept that what we have is derived from this State copy.

Whether or not our texts were affected by what actors did before the decree was passed, what seems incontrovertible is that it must have had as one of its aims to stamp out the practice of interference with the old plays by those who put them on in the festivals in a competition alongside the new. It is not clear why the actors had been doing this.[9] But there are two other ancient sources which seem to confirm that the practice was common and well-known.

Quintilian *Institutio Oratoria* I.10.66 tells us this:

> Tragoedias primus in lucem Aeschylus protulit, sublimis et grauis et grandilocus saepe usque ad uitium, sed rudis in plerisque et incompositus: propter quod correctas eius fabulas in certamen deferre posterioribus poetis Athenienses permisere: suntque eo modo multi coronati.

> As for tragedy, Aeschylus was the first to bring them to the light of day. He was sublime, serious, and high-flown often to a fault, but crude and lacking polish in most parts. This was the reason why the Athenians allowed later poets to enter his plays into the competition in altered versions. Indeed, many won prizes in this way.

Clearly, Quintilian is dependent upon a long tradition here, of which we know scarcely anything. *Vita Aeschyli* 12 tells us that:

---

[8] R. Hamilton, 'Objective Evidence for Actors' Interpolations in Greek Tragedy', *GRBS* 15 (1974), pp. 387-402. See pp. 400-1 for Lycurgus' decree.

[9] A passage in Aristotle's *Politics* (1336b28ff.) suggests that the actor Theodorus altered plays to make certain that he was always the first actor on stage. But the fact that this was observable, if it was, does not necessarily mean Aristotle's explanation is right. It matters far more whether we can find any visible function for tragedy in the *polis* which would make it worthwhile for the actors to expend the energy required to 'workshop' an old play into a different form. See further Keith Sidwell, 'The politics of Aeschylus' *Eumenides*', *Classics Ireland* 3 (1996), pp. 182-203.

Ἀθηναῖοι δὲ τοσοῦτον ἠγάπησαν Αἰσχύλον ὡς
ψηφίσασθαι μετὰ τὸν θάνατον αὐτοῦ τὸν βουλόμενον
διδάσκειν τὰ Αἰσχύλου χορὸν λαμβάνειν

…the Athenians so loved Aeschylus that they passed a decree after his death that whoever wished to produce his plays should be given a chorus.

But there is no mention of the alteration of his plays. We ought to be careful about accepting at face value what Quintilian tells us of the reasons for the Athenians' ecologically unsound attitude to Aeschylus. The *Vita* writer probably did not *know* for sure that it was love of Aeschylus which prompted the decree. Alexandrian writers lived in a world where art was central. Naturally they would have assumed that the information touching on tragedy's regulation by the city reflected a similar value the Athenians placed on the past. The information obtained by Quintilian from some similar source has been subjected to a comparable process of interpretation. However, it must have been known *that* Aeschylus' plays were altered. The easiest way to explain why was to go to another central platform of the Alexandrian literary project, style. Authors who in a sense thought they were improving on Homer would certainly have found it easy to understand (and forgive) later producers of Aeschylus for polishing up his antiquated verses for a more sophisticated public. The true reasons remain obscure. However, the passage leaves us in no doubt that it was well known alterations had been made to Aeschylus' plays. If this information permeated to later antiquity, it must have been common knowledge in the fifth and fourth centuries.

Nonetheless, the remark is rather general. Controversy rages still over what changes we might trace in our surviving texts. One suggestion is that the end of the *Seven Against Thebes* was substituted for the original by a poet/producer who knew Sophocles' *Antigone* and Euripides' *Phoenissae*.[10] It does not perhaps matter whether we agree or disagree with the particular instance. The idea is certainly available that material from other plays might have been inserted in existing plays.

---

[10] See most recently G.O. Hutchinson, *Aeschylus, Seven Against Thebes* (Oxford, 1985), pp. xlii-xliii, and the notes to lines 1005-78, pp. 209-211 for references to earlier discussions.

The final piece of ancient evidence helps us further, though the discussion needs to tread carefully here around some problems of reference and dating. *Anek. Bekk.* 39.19 reports a gloss of Phrynichus:

ἐπικαττύειν καὶ πτερνίζειν τὰ παλαιὰ ἐπισκευάζειν, λέγουσι δ' ἐπὶ τῶν τὰ παλαιὰ τῶν δραμάτων μεταποιούντων καὶ μεταρραπτόντων

putting other soles and heels on old sandals, means restoring the old; they are speaking of those who rework and restitch the old dramas.

Hamilton is inclined to link this with the practice of *contaminatio* "the blending of two Greek originals, to make one new play."[11] However, Phrynichus was a writer of the Second Sophistic, and is most unlikely to have been speaking about *Roman* comedy. Moreover, he is also unlikely to have been commenting on a comic line from anything later than the fourth century BC. It is more reasonable to suppose that Phrynichus here reports a satirical comment from someone who was adverting to precisely the practice we have just looked at as a conjecture in Aeschylus' *Septem*, viz. the insertion of material from elsewhere into an existing drama. Comedy in the fifth century often made fun of tragedy. It is reasonable to suppose that here too the original author was alluding to the practice of altering old tragedies for production at the festivals. The date of the text must lie, then, between 387/6 (the date of the competition in old tragedy at the Dionysia[12]) and c. 338 (date of the Lycurgus decree already cited).

The practice mentioned by Phrynichus makes it possible to suggest an alternative explanation of Aristotle's argument. This now runs:

…embolima are a bad thing. Everyone knows about the practice of altering old plays by inserting speeches or episodes into them from other plays. This practice is universally condemned and has been recently the subject of legislation. Embolima are no different.

---

[11] Hamilton (n. 8) p. 400.

[12] See A. Pickard-Cambridge, *The Dramatic Festivals of Athens²*, revised J. Gould and D.M. Lewis, reissued with new supplement (Oxford, 1988), p. 105 for the text of IG ii² 2318 relating to 387/6 and pp. 72 and 99 for discussion.

There is no way to tell objectively which of these versions is correct. I submit, however, that the interpetation based on the existence of a practice similar to embolima, but universally condemned, makes Aristotle's argument a great deal more weighty.

SOME *EUNAPIANA*

David Woods

The pagan sophist Eunapius of Sardis (347-c.404) composed a *History* which continued the *Chronicle* of Dexippus of Athens from 270 to 404. Unfortunately, it has not itself survived, so we depend for our knowledge of it, first, on its use by later authors, chiefly Zosimus writing c.502, then, on excerpts preserved both in the *Excerpta Historica* compiled under Constantine VII Porphyrogenitus (913-59) and in the late 10th-century lexicon known as the *Suda*, and, finally, on cross-references in Eunapius' other known work, the *Lives of the Sophists*.[1] There is much room fo: controversy, therefore, concerning the accuracy with which these sources preserve Eunapius' own words, or, in some instances, whether they preserve his words at all. Moreover, the nature of our knowledge of this text is such that any larger thesis tends itself to fragment into a series of smaller notes concerning the identification or interpretation of a number of short passages which often have little direct bearing upon one another. The present paper consists of four such notes, the first two revealing the difficulty in recovering what Eunapius himself actually wrote from the words of these later sources, the second two that Eunapius did not always understand his own sources very well. Together, they serve to illustrate the interest of Eunapius as a source both to secular and ecclesiastical historians. The study of a Greek author who has contributed so much to our understanding of late Roman history, a pagan who has contributed to our understanding of the early church, is a fitting tribute, I hope, to the efforts of my former teachers who have contributed so much to my understanding of both the Greek language and Roman history, and to the continuation of patristic scholarship at Maynooth.

I   Constantine I and the *Persocomites*

The 9th century saw an explosion of interest in the life of Constantine I

---

[1] The best introductions to Eunapius and his work consist of two recent doctoral dissertations. See T.M. Banchich, *The Historical Fragments of Eunapius of Sardis* (submitted at the State University of New York at Buffalo, 1985: UMI no. 8528233), and A.E. Baker, *Eunapius and Zosimus: Problems of Composition and Chronology* (submitted at Brown University, 1987: UMI no. 8715450). Texts and translations of the fragments are most easily accessible in R.C. Blockley, *The Fragmentary Classicising Historians of the Later Roman Empire* II (Liverpool, 1983), pp. 2-150.

(306-37) which resulted in the composition of many hagiographical accounts of his life.[2] One of the earliest of these was the Guidi-legend, as it is now called after its modern editor,[3] also referred to as *BHG* 364 from its place within the standard catalogue of hagiographical texts.[4] It shares important similarities with the *Chronicle* of Theophanes Confessor, who died in 818,[5] and it is generally accepted that it was composed during the mid- to late 9th-century also, even if the exact nature of its relationship with the *Chronicle* is a matter of controversy.[6] It is the first surviving life of Constantine to preserve in full a number of features which are commonly found in the later Byzantine lives of Constantine, and its importance in the development of the Constantinian legend is such that it has recently been translated into English.[7] It is the purpose of the present paper to offer a new explanation for the origin of what is probably the most puzzling element in

---

[2] See A. Kazhdan, '"Constantin Imaginaire": Byzantine Legends in the Ninth Century about Constantine the Great', *Byzantion* 57 (1987), pp. 196-250; also S.N.C. Lieu, 'From History to Legend and Legend to History: The Medieval and Byzantine Transformation of Constantine's *Vita*', in S.N.C. Lieu and D. Montserrat (eds.), *Constantine: History, Historiography, and Legend* (London, 1998), pp. 136-76.

[3] See M. Guidi, 'Un ΒΙΟΣ di Constantino', *Rendiconti della Reale accademia dei Lincei, Classe di Scienze Morale, Storiche e Filologiche*, 5th ser. 16 (1907), pp. 304-40 and 637-60.

[4] See F. Halkin (ed.), *Bibliotheca Hagiographica Graeca* I (Brussels, 1957).

[5] In general, see C. Mango and R. Scott (eds.), *The Chronicle of Theophanes Confessor: Byzantine and Near Eastern History AD 284-813* (Oxford, 1997), esp. pp. 24-40.

[6] It seems that the Guidi-legend shares a common source with the *Chronicle* of Theophanes and the undateable *On the Discovery of the True Cross* by one Alexander the Monk. See Mango and Scott (n. 5), p. lxxvii; also R. Scott, 'The Image of Constantine in Malalas and Theophanes', in P. Magdalino (ed.), *New Constantines: The Rhythm of Imperial Renewal in Byzantium, 4th-13th Centuries* (Aldershot, 1994), pp. 57-71, at 67.

[7] Trans. by F. Beetham, with revisions by the editors, in S.N.C. Lieu and D. Montserrat (eds.), *From Constantine to Julian: Pagan and Byzantine Views. A Source History* (London, 1996), pp. 97-146. The translation is extremely welcome, although it contains the odd slip. E.g. on p. 131, the list of confessors who attended the council of Nicaea in 325 should refer to Nicolaus of Myra, a town in Lycia, rather than to "Nicolaus of the unguents." Guidi (n. 3), 638, 1.8 contributed to this error by failing to capitalize Myra (Νικόλαος ὁ τῶν μύρων), although he did so for the other towns named in the same context. *Pace* C. Kelly, *CR* 47 (1997), 436, the inclusion of the "long and lugubriously hagiographical Guidi-Vita" is the most valuable element of this volume, while the translation of the *Artemii Passio*, marred as it is by the decision to omit chs. 25-34, must come a close second. One looks forward to the publication as soon as possible also of Beetham's translation of the so-called Opitz-*Vita* (*BHG* 365).

this text, the alleged capture of Constantine by the Persians.[8]

According to this story, shortly after the death of his father Constantius I
(293-306), Constantine gathered an army of 20,000 men and led them
against the Persians who were attacking Roman cities at that time. Before
any engagement could take place, however, the Persians surprised the
Roman camp in an attack by night, and captured the emperor himself and
many of his staff. The rest of his army was put to flight, some of whom
were pursued as far as the Roman border, but others, those with swift
horses, managed to escape to a tree-covered mountain nearby in Persia
itself. Shortly afterwards the latter group captured some of the Persians'
slaves as they came to cut wood, and asked them what was happening to
their emperor. The slaves told them that the Persians intended to sacrifice
Constantine on the birthday of their gods, the very next day, but they also
agreed to help rescue him in return for their lives. They claimed that the
Persians were vulnerable to attack when they offered sacrifice, since they
left their weapons outside the wall surrounding their altar. So the next day,
when Constantine was dragged bound to the altar, the slaves gave the signal
to the Romans who were hiding nearby, and these seized the Persians'
weapons first before attacking the Persians themselves. The king of the
Persians then fell down before Constantine as he was being released,
begged him to spare his life, and requested a peace-treaty for a fixed period.
Constantine granted these requests, and the Persian king then gave him a
thousand Persian guards also. Constantine returned to Gaul next, from
where he soon launched his attack upon the persecuting emperor Maxentius
which culminated in his victory at the battle of the Milvian bridge.

Clearly, there are huge problems with this story as it stands. In so far as
Constantius I died in 306, and the battle of the Milvian bridge occurred in
312, it seems to require us to believe that Constantine led an expedition
against the Persians sometime during the period 306-12. This would have

---

[8] Guidi (n. 3), 316-19; ch. 7 of the text as divided in Lieu and Montserrat (n. 7), pp. 113-
15. In reference to this aspect of the Constantinian legend, Lieu (n. 2), p. 168, claims that
"echoes of the extraordinarily successful Persian campaigns of Heraclius in the seventh
century are too numerous to mention", and does not care to trouble us with detail. It
remains unclear whether he thinks that these campaigns inspired this aspect of the legend
from its very start, or whether they merely influenced its continued growth as witnessed
to by the so-called Patmos-Vita (*BHG* 365n) of the 12/13th-centuries. If the former is the
case, then I shall be arguing against him here.

been impossible, however, since Constantine only controlled Britain, Gaul and Spain at this time, and would have had to march through the territories of three rival emperors – Maxentius in Italy, Galerius Maximianus in the Balkans, and Maximinus in the East – in order to confront the Persians. Later hagiographers spotted that there was a problem here, and sought to redate this element within the greater Constantinian legend. Hence the anonymous author of the passion of St. Eusignius, a fictitious military martyr allegedly executed by the emperor Julian (360-63), used a life of Constantine similar to the Guidi-legend in order to create a military career for St. Eusignius, even claiming that Eusignius had participated in the rescue of Constantine from the Persians, but he set this event after the discovery of the True Cross in Jerusalem by Constantine's mother Helena, i.e. during the late 320s apparently.[9] Another life of Constantine, the so-called Patmos-legend (*BHG* 365n), seems to envisage a similarly late date for this episode in so far as it sets its version of Constantine's war against the Persians after its accounts of his destruction of the tyrants Maxentius and Licinius, and associates it with his foundation of Constantinople.[10] The problem, however, is that there is no evidence that Constantine ever took to the field against the Persians.[11] True, this does seem to have been his intention at his death in May 337, but he had not yet advanced beyond the preparations for such an expedition when he suddenly died at Nicomedia, far removed from the Persian frontier.[12] So shifting the setting of his alleged capture by the Persians within the greater Constantinian legend does not solve the problem, although the medieval hagiographers were not to know this. For my part, I intend to tackle this problem in two stages. First, I shall re-examine the evidence for the identity of the guards whom the Persian king is alleged to have given to Constantine in order to prove that such a named unit really did exist, even if the legend has distorted its origin. I shall then turn to a broader consideration of the wider episode in order to investigate whether one can detect any historical basis for the episode as a

---

[9] See P. Devos, 'Une Recension Nouvelle de la Passion Grecque *BHG* 639 de Saint Eusignios', *Analecta Bollandiana* 100 (1982), pp. 209-28, at 225-27.

[10] See F. Halkin, 'Une Nouvelle Vie de Constantin dans un Légendier de Patmos', *Analecta Bollandiana* 77 (1959), pp. 63-107, at 84-86.

[11] On Constantine's movements, see T.D. Barnes, *The New Empire of Diocletian and Constantine* (Cambridge, Mass., 1982), pp. 68-80.

[12] See G. Fowden, 'The Last Days of Constantine: Oppositional Versions and Their Influence', *JRS* 84 (1994), pp. 146-70; also D. Woods, 'Where did Constantine I die ?', *JThS* 48 (1997), pp. 531-35.

whole rather than for the individual elements within it.

(a) The Identity of the Persocomites
To begin, therefore, we are fortunate that the Guidi-legend preserves the exact title of the guards whom the Persian king gave to Constantine. The relevant text, and its most recent translation, run as follow:

ὁ δὲ βασιλεὺς τῶν Περσῶν παρέδωκε τῷ βασιλεῖ τῶν
Ῥωμαίων χιλίους Πέρσας φύλακας, οἵτινες καὶ
προσηγορεύθησαν παρὰ τοῦ ἐν ἁγίοις ὡς ἀληθῶς
Κωνσταντίνου Περσοκόμητες.[13]

moreover, the king of the Persians handed over to the emperor of the Romans a thousand Persian guards, who received from Constantine, who is truly one of the saints, the title of the Long-haired Persians.[14]

The passion of St. Eusignius preserves a similar account of the origin of these guards in a speech which it attributes to St. Eusignius during his trial before the emperor Julian:

Τότε ὁ βασιλεὺς τῶν Περσῶν ἀπέθετο ἐν ὅρκῳ εἰρήνην
ἐπὶ ἔτη φανερά, ὡς μὴ ἐπιβουλεῦσαι καθ᾽ ἡμῶν, καὶ
παρέδωκεν ἡμῖν χιλίους Πέρσας φύλακας, οἵτινες
ἐπεκλήθησαν παρ᾽ ἡμῶν καὶ τοῦ βασιλέως Περσοκόμιτες.
Καὶ ἐστιν ἄχρι τοῦ νῦν ὁ ἀριθμὸς τῶν χιλίων
φυλάττοντες τοὺς ὅρους Ῥωμαίων τε καὶ Περσῶν.[15]

Then the king of the Persians made a peace-treaty for a fixed number of years, that he would not plot against us, and he surrendered to us a thousand Persian guards, whom we and the emperor have called the Persian Companions. And this unit of a thousand men has remained guarding the borders of the Romans and the Persians until the present time.[16]

---

[13] Guidi (n. 3), 319, l.1-3.
[14] Lieu and Montserrat (n. 7), p. 115.
[15] Devos (n. 9), 226-27.
[16] My translation. Kazhdan (n. 2), 204, fails to note that it is Eusignius who claims that

My first point is that the title of these Persian guards should be translated as the 'Persian Companions' rather than the 'Long-haired Persians'. The prefix *Perso-* has been added to the plural of the Latin noun *comes* 'companion', i.e. *comites*, rather than to the plural of the Greek adjective κομήτης 'long-haired', i.e. κομῆται. Some confusion is possible not only because the stem of the Latin noun is variously transliterated into Greek either as κόμιτ- (e.g. κόμιτα) or κόμητ- (e.g. κόμητα), but also because the ancient Persians had been described as 'long-haired' on at least one famous occasion.[17] It is clear from the context, however, that we are dealing here with a transliteration of the Latin *comites* rather than a variant spelling of the Greek κομῆται. First, the Guidi-legend preserves many terms which are transliterations into Greek of original Latin terms, of military terms in particular. These include the terms τριβοῦνος (Lat. *tribunus*), φοσσάτον (Lat. *fossatum*), βίγλα (Lat. *vigilia*), κάστρον (Lat. *castra*), and λιβέλλος (Lat. *libellus*).[18] It is no surprise, therefore, to discover another instance of this phenomenon. More importantly, though, and as I will discuss next, the Latin *comites* was used as a military title in the late Roman army in the exact fashion that it occurs here in the Guidi-legend. Hence there can be no doubt that the title Περσοκόμητες ought best to be translated as 'Persian Companions'.

The use of *comites* 'companions' as a formal military title in the Roman army seems to date to the late 3rd-century. A papyrus text reveals that troops described as the κομίτες τοῦ κυρίου 'companions of the Lord' were present in Egypt with the emperor Galerius Maximianus in 295, while an undated inscription of approximately the same period records the deaths in Italy of two brothers who were members of the *comites imperatoris* 'companions of the emperor'.[19] Our best source in this matter is the *Notitia*

---

the *Persocomites* were still guarding the borders in his present, i.e. in 362, not the anonymous author of the passion, so there is no need to accept this statement at its face value as he does, that the *Persocomites* were ever really set guarding any border. This element represents an addition to the original source by the author of the passion. Nor does Kazhdan explain his claim that "this institution of border guardians may recall the situation on the Arab frontier rather than that on the Persian."

[17] Herodotus 6.19.

[18] Respectively, Guidi (n. 3), 310, l.14; 313, l.27; 316, l.13; 637, l.17; 641, l.8.

[19] *P. Oxy.* 43; *CIL* 11.6168. M.P. Speidel, *Riding for Caesar: The Roman Emperors'*

Dignitatum, a composite document whose detailed accounts of all the military units in the eastern and western halves of the empire have been dated c.401 and c.420 respectively.[20] It preserves the names of 11 units which bore the title *comites*, and these all served as cavalry units, vexillations to be precise, the majority as *vexillationes palatinae*,[21] two as *vexillationes comitatenses*.[22] The titles of two of the *vexillationes palatinae*, the *comites Arcadiaci* (*Or.* 8.25) and the *comites Honoriaci* (*Or.* 8.26), named after the emperors Arcadius (383-408) and Honorius (393-423) respectively, reveal that new units of this title were still being created by the end of the 4th-century even, and it remains possible that further such units were created in the centuries that followed. As far as we are here concerned, not only does the *Notitia Dignitatum* fail to name the *Persocomites* as such, but it fails to name any unit at all whose titles included the prefix *Perso-*. Indeed, the only units we know whose titles included this prefix were creations of Justinian I (527-65), the *equites Perso-Justiniani* and the *felices Perso-Armenii*.[23] These units were both stationed in Italy for a time, and had presumably been formed of prisoners whom the Romans had captured during Justinian's Persian war.[24]

It is a distinct possibility, therefore, that the *Persocomites*, if they had ever existed at all, were another Justinianic creation also. Yet such an interpretation of the evidence places too great an emphasis on the exact form of the title as presently preserved. The *Notitia Dignitatum* itself illustrates that a certain flexibility had come to exist in this matter by the end of the 4th-century at latest. It often refers to the same unit twice under different headings, and sometimes changes the details of their titles as it does so. For example, the *equites sagittarii Parthi seniores* occur as such on

---

Horse Guard (London, 1994), p. 199, n. 188, suggests that the brothers may have arrived in Italy with Galerius Maximianus in 307.

[20] On the dating problem, see J.C. Mann, 'The *Notitia Dignitatum* - Dating and Survival', *Britannia* 22 (1991), pp. 215-19; also C. Zuckerman, 'Comtes et ducs en Égypte autour de l'an 400 et la date de la *Notitia Dignitatum Orientis*', *Antiquité Tardive* 6 (1998), pp. 137-47.

[21] *comites clibanarii* (*Or.* 5.29); *comites sagittarii iuniores* (Or. 5.30); *comites Taifali* (*Or.* 5.31); *comites seniores* (*Or.* 6.28); *comites sagittarii Armeni* (*Or.* 6.31); *comites Arcadiaci* (*Or.* 8.25); *comites Honoriaci* (*Or.* 8.26); *comites seniores* (*Oc.* 6.43); *comites Alani* (*Oc.* 6.50).

[22] *comites catafractarii bucellarii iuniores* (*Or.* 7.25); *comites iuniores* (*Oc.* 6.75).

[23] *ILS* 2810; *P. Dip.* 122.

[24] Procopius, *Bella* 2.19.24-25.

one occasion (*Oc.* 6.68), but as the *equites Parthosagittarii seniores* on another (*Oc.* 7.186).[25] The tendency to run the ethnic title of a unit into one of its other titles, and treat it as a prefix, is evident from the papyrological evidence also. A certain Flavius Abinnaeus has left us an account of his career in which he claims that he served in the *vexillatio Parthusagittariorum* at Diospolis in the province of Thebais, for 33 years apparently c.303-36.[26] The *Notitia* refers to the same unit simply as the *equites sagittarii indigenae* (*Or.* 31.27), from which it is clear that the title *Parthusagittarii* represents a running together of the separate titles *sagittarii* and *Parthi*, exactly as in the previous example. It is arguable, therefore, that the title *Persocomites* represents a similar such transformation. In order to restore the full formal titles of this unit as they most probably were had it existed in the 4th century, we must separate out its ethnic title once more. In this manner, the *Persocomites* become the *comites Persae*. But does the evidence support the existence of the *comites Persae* any more than it does that of the *Persocomites*?

An examination of the *Notitia* reveals only one unit which included *Persae* among its titles, a *vexillatio palatina* entitled the *equites Persae clibanarii* (*Or.* 6.32). It also reveals that there were only two *vexillationes palatinae* which included *clibanarii* among their titles, the same *equites Persae clibanarii* and the *comites clibanarii* (*Or.* 5.29). It has long been recognised that most late Roman military units, of the mobile armies at least, were created and/or operated in pairs, and that this was true of the *vexillationes palatinae* also.[27] The organization of the Roman army changed a great deal as the 4th century progressed, and Theodosius I (379-95) deliberately broke many old pairings during his reorganization of his mobile forces. Nevertheless, it remains a relatively simple task to reconstruct the pairs, or 'brigades', in which most of the eastern *vexillationes palatinae* surviving

---

[25] O. Seeck (ed.), *Notitia Dignitatum* (Berlin, 1876), p. 141, amends *Oc.* 7.186 to read *equites Parthi_sagittarii seniores*. But his *apparatus criticus* reveals that the four main manuscripts all read *Panthosagittarii* which seems better restored as *Parthosagittarii* rather than *Parthi sagittarii*.

[26] *P. Abinn.* 1.4-5: '... *traditus in vexillatione Parthusagittariorum degentium Diospoli provincia[e] T[h]e[ba]i[d]os super[i]oris*'. See T.D. Barnes, 'The Career of Abinnaeus', *Phoenix* 39 (1985), pp. 368-74.

[27] E.g. see R.S.O. Tomlin, '*Seniores-Iuniores* in the Late Roman Field Army', *AJPh* 93 (1972), pp. 253-78, esp. n. 10; also H. Elton, *Warfare in Roman Europe AD 350-425* (Oxford, 1996), p. 91.

c.401 had originally served, on the basis of their status, titles, and their relative positions within the relevant lists. My reconstructions of these pairs run as follows:[28]

(*Or.* 5.28) *equites promoti seniores*	(*Or.* 6.28) *comites seniores*
(*Or.* 5.29) *comites clibanarii*	(*Or.* 6.32) *equites Persae clibanarii*
(*Or.* 5.30) *comites sagittarii iuniores*	(*Or.* 6.31) *comites sagittarii Armeni*
(*Or.* 5.31) *comites Taifali*	(*Oc.* 6.50) *comites Alani*
(*Or.* 5.32) *equites Arcades*	(*Oc.*6.52) *equites Constantes Valentinianenses seniores*
(*Or.* 6.29) *equites Brachiati iuniores*	(*Oc.* 6.49) *equites Cornuti iuniores*
(*Or.* 6.33) *equites Theodosiaci seniores*	(*Or.* 8.27) *equites Theodosiaci iuniores*
(*Or.* 8.25) *comites Arcadiaci*	(*Or.* 8.26) *comites Honoriaci*

It would seem, therefore, if for no other reason than by a process of elimination, that the *comites clibanarii* had probably been paired with the *equites Persae clibanarii* originally.

It is important next to note that the *Notitia* sometimes omits elements from the full formal titles of the units which it lists. For example, units from various Gallic cities appear as the most senior *vexillationes comitatenses* subject to the two eastern *magistri militum praesentales* and the *magister militum per Thracias*. These have been identified as units which Constantius II transferred to the East following his defeat of the western usurper Magnentius in 353.[29] The first *magister militum praesentalis* had as his most senior *vexillatio comitatensis* the *equites catafractarii Biturigenses* (*Or.* 5.34), the second *magister militum praesentalis* had as his two most senior units the *equites catafractarii* (*Or.* 6.35) and the *equites catafractarii Ambianenses* (*Or.* 6.36), and the *magister militum per Thracias* had as his most senior unit of this type the *equites catafractarii Albigenses* (*Or.* 8.29). It is immediately clear that its final title has been lost in the case of the *equites catafractarii* (*Or.* 6.35). By good luck, however, an epitaph from Heraclea Lyncestis preserves the full titles of a unit entitled the *equites catafractarii Pictavenses*.[30] It has been argued, therefore, that the full titles of the *equites catafractarii* (*Or.* 6.35) should be restored as the *equites catafractarii Pictavenses*.[31] A second inscription reinforces this point. The

---

[28] There remains one unit whose original partner seems to have been lost, probably at the battle of Adrianopolis in 378, the *equites Batavi iuniores* (*Or.* 6.30).

[29] See D. Hoffmann, *Das spätrömische Bewegungsheer und die Notitia Dignitatum* I (Düsseldorf, 1969), pp. 484-85.

[30] *CIL* 3.14406a.

[31] Hoffmann (n. 29), p. 493.

epitaph of Flavius Aemilianus, which is securly dated to 356, records that he had served as a member of the *Io[viani] Cor[nuti] sen[iores]*.[32] The *Notitia* does not list any unit by these exact titles, but it does list units entitled the *Ioviani seniores* (*Oc.* 5.145) and the *Cornuti seniores* (*Oc.* 5.158).[33] This suggests that one of these is identifiable as the unit in which Aemilianus had served, but that the *Notitia* has failed to preserve its full titles. Finally, the *Notitia* refers to the garrison at Hermopolis in Egypt as the *cuneus equitum scutariorum* (*Or.* 31.24) while the papyrological evidence proves that its full title should have read *cuneus equitum Maurorum scutariorum*.[34] It is evident, therefore, that the *Notitia* does not necessarily preserve the full and correct titles of every unit which it lists, and we cannot simply assume this in the case of the *comites clibanarii*, certainly not if there is any evidence to the contrary.

Finally, the description of the *comites clibanarii* as a unit of *clibanarii* provides strong grounds to believe that it was of eastern origin. First, the Romans perceived that one of the strengths of the Persian army was its heavy-armoured cavalry, its *clibanarii*, and the only theatre of operations where they may have felt under pressure to develop the same type of cavalry as a counter-measure was along the eastern front.[35] Next, the *Notitia*

---

[32] See T. Drew-Bear, 'A Fourth Century Latin Soldier's Epitaph at Nakolea', *HSCPh* 81 (1977), pp. 257-74. The restoration of the first title, whether it should read *Io[viani]* or *Io[vii]*, is somewhat controversial. M.P. Speidel, 'Raising New Units for the Late Roman Army: *Auxilia Palatina*', *DOP* 50 (1996), pp. 163-70, prefers *Iovii*, but his argument rests on a misinterpretation of Aur. Vict. *Caes.* 39.15 which refers to units named after *both* Maximianus as Herculius and Diocletian as Iovius. But since there were no units entitled *Herculii* analogous to those entitled *Iovii*, he must refer to the units entitled *Herculiani* and *Ioviani*. Furthermore, it is important to remember that Victor was not writing a military manual, and does not necessarily use the term *auxilium* in its technical sense, so there is no reason to assume that the units to which he was referring were *auxilia palatina* rather than legions. In the present context, however, it matters little whether we restore the full titles of this unit as *Ioviani Cornuti seniores* or *Iovii Cornuti seniores*, since the *Notitia* does not record any unit with either set of titles in full.
[33] Alternatively, it also lists a unit entitled the *Iovii seniores* (*Oc.* 5.168).
[34] See J.G. Keenan, 'Soldier and Civilian in Byzantine Hermopolis', in A. Bülow-Jacobsen, *Proceedings of the 20th International Congress of Papyrologists* (Copenhagen, 1994), pp. 444-51, esp. n. 3.
[35] See J.W. Eadie, 'The Development of Roman Mailed Cavalry', *JRS* 57 (1967), pp. 161-73; M.P. Speidel, '*Catafractarii Clibanarii* and the Rise of Later Roman Mailed Cavalry: A Gravestone from Claudiopolis in Bithynia', *Epigraphica Anatolica* 4 (1984), pp. 151-56. Armoured cavalry from, or in, the West, tended to take the form of *catafractarii*

lists only nine units which included the term *clibanarii* among their titles, and eight of these were situated within the eastern armies.[36] Furthermore, of these nine units, the eastern origin of five are explicit in their titles, three being described as *Parthi*, one as *Persae*, and one as *Palmyreni*. None were obviously of western origin, since the four remaining units lacked any ethnic title at all. Not surprisingly, the workshops which produced their armour for the *clibanarii* were also situated mostly in the East.[37] There is strong reason to suspect, therefore, that the four units of *clibanarii* listed without ethnic titles were themselves of eastern origin also, and that, if they are ever recovered, their titles will probably be found to be similar to those already noted - *Parthi, Persae,* or *Palmyreni*.

In this manner, therefore, the association of the *comites clibanarii* with the *equites Persae clibanarii*, the proven fallibility of the *Notitia* in the matter of the preservation of the full titles of any unit, and the apparent eastern orign of the *clibanarii*, all combine to suggest that the full title of the *comites clibanarii* was the *comites [Persae] clibanarii*.

The identification of our *Persocomites* as the *comites [Persae] clibanarii* of the *Notitia* suggests only that our hagiographical sources are correct that such a unit did exist. But did it exist under Constantine I? Although our literary sources do not always maintain a proper distinction between the terms *Parthi* and *Persae*,[38] the use of *Persae* seems *prima facie* evidence at least that this unit was created sometime after the replacement by the

---

rather than *clibanarii*, i.e. the horses lacked the mail protection of their riders.

[36] *comites clibanarii* (*Or.* 5.29); *equites primi clibanarii Parthi* (*Or.* 5.40); *equites Persae clibanarii* (*Or.* 6.32); *equites secundi clibanarii Parthi* (*Or.* 6.40); *equites promoti clibanarii* (*Or.* 7.31); *equites quarti clibanarii Parthi* (*Or.* 7.32); *cuneus equitum secundorum clibanariorum Palmyrenorum* (*Or.* 7.34); *schola scutariorum clibanariorum* (*Or.* 11.8); *equites sagittarii clibanarii* (*Oc.* 6.67 = *Oc.* 7.185). The fact that the only western unit of *clibanarii* was stationed in Africa may be of some significance in so far as this was the region where the conditions most resembled those of the eastern frontier.

[37] *Fabricae clibanariae* were situated in the East at Antioch (*Or.* 11.22), Caesarea in Cappadocia (*Or.* 11.26), and Nicomedia (*Or.* 11.28). One was also situated at Augustodunum in Gaul (*Oc.* 9.33). See S. James, 'The *Fabricae*: State Arms Factories of the Later Roman Empire', in J.C. Coulston (ed.), *Military Equipment and the Identity of Roman Soldiers* (Oxford, 1988), pp. 257-331, at 261-65.

[38] See A. Chauvot, 'Parthes et Perses dans les sources du IVe siècle', in M. Christol *et alii* (eds.), *Institutions, Société, et Vie Politique dans l'Empire Romain au IVe Siècle ap. J.C.* (Rome, 1992), pp. 115-25.

Persian Sassanids of the Parthian Arsacids as the ruling dynasty of Iran, i.e. after 224. Two facts point to the creation of the *comites [Persae] clibanarii* during the early 4th-century in particular. First, the fact that it occurs only second after the *equites promoti seniores* (*Or.* 5.29) in the list of *vexillationes palatinae* subject to the first eastern *magister militum praesentalis* points to its relative seniority, and early creation, therefore. Second, the *comites [Persae] clibanarii* form a pair with the *equites Persae clibanarii* in the exact manner that the *comites seniores* (*Or.* 6.28) form a pair with the *equites promoti seniores* (*Or.* 5.29), i.e. a *comites – equites* pair, the only two such among all the pairs of *vexillationes palatinae*. This suggests that these two pairs of units were created either at the same time or one in imitation of the other. It has been argued that the *comites seniores* and the *equites promoti seniores* were formed from the *equites singulares Augusti* and the praetorian horse respectively, and if this had not already occurred under Diocletian (284-305), then it had certainly occurred by the time that Constantine disbanded the praetorian guard in 312.[39] The evidence suggests, therefore, that the *comites [Persae] clibanarii* and the *equites Persae clibanarii* were created in imitation of the *comites seniores* and the *equites promoti seniores*, and in so far as the latter seem to have originated under Diocletian, then the former must date to that period also, or sometime thereafter. But there is no good reason yet to associate their creation with the reign of Constantine I in particular.

So far we have focussed on the use of the title *comites*, but the description of the *Persocomites*, or *comites Persae*, as *Persae*, i.e. Persians, is equally important. The description of a newly created unit in this manner suggests that it was formed of Persians, so the question now is when, if ever, during the early 4th-century were Persians either available or acceptable as recruits into the Roman army? The Persian frontier had remained relatively quiet since the treaty of 299 following Galerius Maximianus' smashing victory over the Persian king Narses and open warfare was not renewed until shortly before the death of Constantine in 337. We are reasonably well informed about the terms of the treaty of 299, and there is no evidence to suggest that it required the Persians to surrender recruits for service in the

---

[39] See M.P. Speidel, 'The Later Roman Field Army and the Guard of the High Empire', *Latomus* 46 (1987), 375-79; *idem*, 'Maxentius' Praetorians', *MEFRA* 100 (1988), pp. 183-86.

Roman army.[40] Certainly, Rome normally insisted that its newly defeated enemies should submit in this manner, but Rome's relationship with Persia was on a different plane. It has been noted, for example, that only in the case of Persia was Rome prepared to exchange hostages, and that this exchange of hostages was a short-term measure pending the negotiation or implementation of a peace-treaty rather than a condition of the peace-treaty itself.[41] Given that Persia did not usually surrender long-term hostages to Rome, even at its darkest moment in 299, it is most improbable that it ever surrendered any recruits for service in Rome's armies. For this reason, it seems unlikely that Galerius Maximianus, or any other emperor, formed the *comites Persae clibanarii* of Persian recruits surrendered for this purpose, as our hagiographical sources would have us believe. The alternative possibilities are that this unit was formed of volunteers, of Persians who had deserted their own state for personal or political reasons, or that it was formed of captives, either of former Persian soldiers or of fresh recruits from a captive civilian base.

As far as Constantine is concerned, he never went to war with Persia, so he never had the opportunity to acquire sufficient captives from which to recruit two fresh units, the *comites Persae* and its sister unit the *equites Persae clibanarii*. On the other hand, he did welcome the Persian prince Hormisdas to his court as a refugee c.324, and one may suspect that Hormisdas brought a small entourage with him.[42] The steady trickle of refugees, traders and adventurers back and forth across the Romano-Persian border may also have contributed to the availability of a small pool of Persian manpower within the Roman borders.[43] But a palatine vexillation probably consisted of about 500 men,[44] so that the creation of the two new units of *Persae* would have required about 1,000 men, and it is difficult to

---

[40] See R.C. Blockley, 'The Roman-Persian Peace Treaties of AD299 and 363', *Florilegium* 6 (1984), pp. 28-49.

[41] See A.D. Lee, 'The Role of Hostages in Roman Diplomacy with Sassanian Persia', *Historia* 40 (1991), pp. 366-74.

[42] Zosimus, *HN* 2.27; Zonaras, *Ann.* 13.5. One notes, though, that John of Antioch, *frag.* 178 in C. Müller, *Fragmenta Historicorum Graecorum* IV (Paris, 1851), p. 605, identifies the emperor who received Hormisdas as Licinius.

[43] See S.N.C. Lieu, 'Captives, Refugees, and Exiles: A Study of Cross-Frontier Civilian Movements and Contacts between Rome and Persia from Valerian to Jovian', in P. Freeman and D. Kennedy (eds.), *The Defence of the Roman and Byzantine East* (Oxford, 1986), pp. 475-505.

[44] See T. Coello, *Unit Sizes in the Late Roman Army* (Oxford, 1996), p. 41.

believe that Hormisdas could have brought so many able-bodied men with him, such were the circumstances of his defection, or that there were so many able-bodied Persians already available within the empire. In short, it is difficult to understand how Constantine could ever have gathered sufficient Persians to justify the inclusion of the title *Persae* among the titles of two new palatine vexillations.

(b) The Creation of the Persocomites in Context
It is now clear that there is a strong argument for identifying the *Persocomites* of the Guidi-legend with a known, historical unit, the *comites [Persae] clibanarii* of the *Notitia Dignitatum*. Unfortunately, though, the *comites [Persae] clibanarii* are little more than a name to us, and we have nothing with which to compare the wider story behind the creation of the *Persocomites* as preserved by the Guidi-legend in order to determine whether it has any historical basis at all. Yet it is not unfair to assume that there must have been some sort of historical basis to it originally, however distorted it may have become in its transmission. We should not underestimate the professional integrity of the medieval Byzantine hagiographer of Constantine, even if we cannot always admire his competence, since as far as Constantine was concerned, he was as much a historian as a hagiographer, and had a wide range of sources upon which to draw. For example, the anonymous author of the Guidi-legend mentions two of his sources by name, bishop Eusebius of Caesarea and his succesor Gelasius, and even if he did not consult their works directly himself, they still remain the ultimate sources for much of the information which he preserves, the sources of his source.[45] Nowhere is this more obvious than in his account of Constantine's vision and his subsequent creation of the *labarum* which clearly derives from Eusebius of Caesarea's original account of the same.[46] He also excuses his failure to detail the honours accorded Constantine at his death on the grounds that such information was easily available in the 'chronicles of the masses'.[47] Hence one suspects that there must have been some sort of historical basis to the wider tale concerning Constantine's war against the Persians which resulted in the creation of the *Persocomites*, and that it was not a complete and deliberate

---

[45] Guidi (n. 3), 319, l. 22; 320, l. 1.
[46] See Lieu and Montserrat (n. 7), p. 143, on Eusebius, *VC* 1.30-31 and Guidi (n. 3), pp. 322-23.
[47] Guidi (n. 3), 654, l. 21.

act of fiction.

Rather than trying to force this tale to fit in with the known facts of Constantine's life, one should consider it in isolation and on its own merits. If we did not already 'know' that it related to Constantine I, to whose reign would we attribute this tale as a somewhat distorted and exaggerated version of a genuine sequence of historical events? One cannot help but note a startling resemblance to the early reign of Constantius II (337-61). It is unfortunate that no full, narrative account of the early reign of Constantius II has survived, since the surviving books of the *Res Gestae* of Ammianus Marcelinus only begin in late 353. Nevertheless, it is possible to see in our account of Constantine's war against the Persians a somewhat confused account of the early reign of Constantius II c.337-44. The similarities may be treated under four headings.

First, the Guidi-legend claims that Constantine I collected an army for use against the Persians shortly after the death of his father. Following his attendance at the funeral of his father Constantine I at Constantinople in May 337 and the subsequent negotiations with his brothers concerning the division of the empire, Constantius II returned to Antioch in Syria for the winter of 337/38 from where he launched a series of campaigns against the Persians and their allies beginning in the spring of 338.[48] The Guidi-legend also makes it clear that the Persians were already attacking Roman cities in the East before Constantine had collected his army against them, and one may see in this a reference to the first siege of Nisibis in 336, if not the destruction of Amida and Antoninopolis also, before Constantine I had died even.[49]

---

[48] On Constantius' movements, see T.D. Barnes, *Athanasius and Constantius: Theology and Politics in the Constantinian Empire* (Cambridge, Mass., 1993), pp. 219-24.

[49] For a full list, and translations, of all the relevant sources for Constantius II's early wars with the Persians, see M.H. Dodgeon and S.N.C. Lieu (eds.), *The Roman Eastern Frontier and the Persian Wars AD 226-363. A Documentary History* (London, 1991), pp. 164-210. Although the sources (e.g. Jerome, *Chron. s.a.* 338) date the first siege of Nisibis to 338, R.W. Burgess, *Studies in Eusebian and Post-Eusebian Chronography* (Stuttgart, 1999), pp. 232-38 (='The Dates of the First Siege of Nisibis and the Death of James of Nisibis', *Byzantion* 69 (1999), pp. 7-17), argues that it occurred in 337, on the basis of his reconstruction of a hypothetical source common to Jerome and other chroniclers, his so-called *Continuatio Antiochiensis*. While Burgess is correct to posit the existence of a common source, he has failed to note that, for the late reign of Constantine I, it systematically postdated events by 2 years, as revealed, for example, by the fact that

Second, the Guidi-legend claims that Constantine was captured in a night-attack by the Persians. According to surviving historical sources, Romans and Persians fought nine major engagements during the reign of Constantius II, although the emperor himself was personally present at only two of these.[50] But he was present at one of the more notorious of these engagements, the famous night-battle at Eleia near Singara, when Roman troops stormed the Persian camp itself, but threw away their victory by continuing to fight in the darkness, so allowing the Persians to mount a successful counter-attack. The details of this battle are obscure because our two main sources for it are the two panegyrics which Libanius and Julian Caesar delivered in 344/45 and 355 respectively.[51] Their prime concern was to prove that the Romans did not really lose this battle, but that if they did lose, it was the fault of the soldiers, and not of the emperor. They put the best possible gloss on events from the Roman perspective, and one notes that they say very little about the exact sequence of events following the Persian counter-attack. The two sides disengaged the next day, and the Persians did retreat back across the Tigris, but it is not at all clear whether they had not managed to recapture their camp on the night. Whatever the case, there is a clear parallel between Constantine's alleged defeat by the Persians during a night-attack and Constantius II's defeat during the night-battle near Singara in 344.[52]

Third, the most incredible element in the Guidi-legend is the claim that Constantine was actually captured by the Persians, although he did manage to escape. There is no evidence that Constantius II was ever captured by the Persians, and it seems most unlikely that he was, but he may have come far closer to capture than the surviving panegyrical accounts of his early wars with Persia would have us believe. Ammianus preserves an intriguing reference to an occasion on which Constantius was defeated in battle by the

---

Jerome dates the death of the empress Fausta to 328 rather than to 326, and the consecration of Athanasius as bishop of Alexandria to 330 rather than to 328. Hence one must deduct 2 years from 338 to discover the correct date of the siege, 336.

[50] Jerome, *Chron. s.a.* 348; Festus, *Brev.* 27.

[51] Libanius, *Or.* 59.103-20; Julian, *Or.* 1.22d-25b.

[52] There is some dispute concerning the date of the battle, since some sources date it to 348 rather than 344, but these seem to have confused two different battles near Singara. The decisive testimony must be that by Julian, *Or.* 1.26b, who claims that the emperor Constans (337-50) died about 6 years after the battle.

Persians and fled with a small group of companions to the safety of an unguarded frontier post where he was forced to live on a meagre allowance of bread supplied to him by a local woman.[53] We cannot date this incident other than to say it must have occurred during the period 338-50, but the fact that Constantius participated personally in the relevant battle, and that he only participated in two of the nine major battles with the Persians during his reign, one of which was the night-battle near Singara, encourages the suspicion that this anecdote relates to the immediate aftermath of his defeat at Singara. Whatever the case, Constantius was separated from the bulk of his forces on at least one occasion following his defeat by the Persians, during which time there must have been a very real fear that he had been either captured or killed.

Finally, the claim by the Guidi-legend that the king of the Persians gave a thousand guards to Constantine, whom he then named his *Persocomites*, is no more credible than the claim that the Persians had captured Constantine. Stepping back from the particulars, however, the broader claim is that Constantine created the *Persocomites* following an earlier defeat by the Persians. Again, this is reminiscent of developments under Constantius II who was forced to reform the cavalry branch of his army in the wake of setbacks against the Persians.[54] In particular, one notes that he was responsible for the creation of some formations of heavy-armed cavalry, *clibanarii*.[55] So there is a parallel between Constantine's alleged creation of the *Persocomites*, whom we have already identified as the *comites* [*Persae*] *clibanarii*, and Constantius II's development of *clibanarii* among his forces also.

It is my argument, therefore, that the story of the Persian war in which Constantine was taken captive is no more than a displaced and distorted account of the earliest phase of the wars between Constantius II and Sapor II of Persia (309-79). That such displacement could, and did, occur is evidenced by the fact that Theophanes Confessor, or a source which he copied, attributed the Persian war which Constantius II waged as Augustus to his period as Caesar under Constantine I, to the ridiculously early year of

---

[53] Amm. 25.9.3.
[54] Hoffmann (n. 29), pp. 265-77.
[55] Julian, *Or.* 1.37c-d.

325 to be precise.[56] Different factors may have contributed to such displacement in different sources, but in this instance it is relatively easily explained. It seems to have resulted from a simple confusion between the names of Constantine I and Constantius II which is all too common in the manuscripts of our surviving sources for late antiquity, whether in Greek or Latin, because only one letter distinguishes between these names in either language. The author of the Guidi-legend, or of a slightly earlier life of Constantine, discovered a source which seemed to tell how Constantine I had launched an expedition against the Persians immediately after the death of his father, and simply copied the relevant excerpt into a pre-existing framework at what he thought was the appropriate point, the description of how Constantine I came to power after the death of his father Constantius I. The apparent distortion or exaggeration in this tale is rather less easy to explain because insufficient comparative material survives from the relevant period, but it is not difficult to envisage how important distinctions in an original account which stated merely that it had been *feared*, or *rumoured*, that Constantius II had himself been captured in the aftermath of a defeat, because of his separation from the main body of his troops for a period, may have been lost in subsequent condensations of a longer and more complex work. This may then have paved the way for the more fantastic inventions. But there is no way of distinguishing whether these elements were already present in the tale before it was salvaged for re-use in a life of Constantine, or represent subsequent developments in the new setting.

It is important to point out that the confusion between the names of Constantine I and Constantius II in this particular instance had occurred long before the composition of the Guidi-legend in the 9th century. In the *Chronicle* which he composed not long after the death of Justinian I in 565,[57] John Malalas describes a victory by Constantine I over the Persians which is clearly an extreme abbreviation of the episode which has been best

---

[56] Theophanes, *Chron.* AM 5815. I will argue elsewhere that the notice at the heart of this entry had originally described the defection of Hormisdas to the Roman empire 322/24, but that by the time Theophanes came to copy the chronicle within which it was embedded, it had become thoroughly corrupted and changed completely, not least because it had been 'corrected' or added to by editors influenced by their knowledge of subsequent events c.336-50.

[57] See E. Jeffreys, B. Croke, and R. Scott (eds.), *Studies in John Malalas* (Sydney, 1990), pp. 1-27.

preserved by the Guidi-legend:

> He [Constantine] began a campaign against the Persians, was
> victorious and made a peace treaty with Sapor, the emperor of
> the Persians. It was the Persians who asked to have peace with
> the Romans.[58]

This raises a question concerning the nature of Malalas' immediate source
in this matter, and its relationship to the Guidi-legend. Was it an early life
of Constantine, and if so was it an ancestor of the Guidi-legend? If it was a
life of Constantine, then its order of events must have been different to that
surviving in the Guidi-legend, since Malalas records Constantine's
campaign against the Persians after his alleged baptism by bishop Silvester
in Rome, whereas the Guidi-legend sets it before his baptism by Silvester. It
is noteworthy, however, that Malalas' account of the life and works of
Constantine is a strange collection of obscure, often unique, facts which
seem to have been dragged together from a number of different sources, and
his account of Constantine's Persian campaign seems to constitute yet
another of these isolated pieces of information rather than part of a larger
life of Constantine. Hence I am inclined to believe that Malalas and the
author of the Guidi-legend both chanced upon the same account of
Constantine's Persian expedition which had been preserved independently
of any life of Constantine as such.

The ultimate source for this episode must remain a mystery, although we do
have two clues. First, the preservation of such a technical detail as the name
of a particular military unit, the *Persocomites*, suggests that it is a narrative
history rather than a rhetorical work, some speech or panegyric, which lies
at the heart of the present mystery, since the latter tend to omit such detail.
Furthermore, the length of the episode, even if it has grown a little during
its transmission, suggests that this history was a full and detailed work
rather than some chronicle or *breviarium*. More importantly, however, the
story does not reflect well on the emperor, even in its present
hagiographical context. The rescue of the emperor is credited to the valour
of his soldiers, or to the slaves of the Persians even, rather to any merit on
his part. The author responsible for the preservation of this unflattering

---

[58] Malalas, *Chron.* 13.3. Trans. by E. Jeffreys *et alii*, *The Chronicle of John
Malalas* (Melbourne, 1986), p. 172.

anecdote was clearly hostile to the emperor concerned, even if the anecdote has become a little exaggerated in the retelling. So we are looking for the author of a detailed political history, which included the reign of Constantius II, but who was hostile to this emperor at least. Hence Eunapius of Sardis must emerge as the strongest candidate in this matter. He wrote a detailed political history which covered the period from 270 to 404, and was a bitter critic of the Christian emperors from Constantine I onwards.[59] As noted above, his history has not itself survived, but many fragments have been preserved in compilations produced under the emperor Constantine Porphyrogenitus. It is generally agreed also that when Zosimus wrote his *New History* c.502, he merely abbreviated large parts of Eunapius' earlier history for much of his account of 4th-century events.[60] In the present context, however, it is noteworthy that no fragments have survived which tell us anything concerning Eunapius' treatment of the earliest wars between Constantius II and Sapor c.337-44. And Zosimus is no more enlightening. He fails to describe any events anywhere in the empire between the death of Constantine II in 340 and that of Constans in 350. He then summarizes over ten years of war on the eastern frontier in a most brief and misleading fashion.[61] For these reasons, we remain almost completely ignorant as to how Eunapius described the Persian wars c.337-50, other than that he characterized them as a defeat for Constantius II. So nothing precludes the identification of Eunapius as the original source for the episode under discussion here. Indeed, the fact that Zosimus preserves an account of the creation of units entitled *Salii* and *Batavi* under Julian Caesar in Gaul c.358,[62] suggests that such detail was of interest to Eunapius, and provides a parallel for the inclusion of similar detail by him also in the case of the *Persocomites*.

Some minor points remain. It must also be said in favour of the

---

[59] See R.C. Blockley, *The Fragmentary Classicising Historians of the Later Roman Empire* I (Liverpool, 1981), pp. 1-26.

[60] E.g. see R.T. Ridley, 'Zosimus the Historian', *Byzantinische Zeitschrift* 65 (1972), pp. 277-302. Baker (n. 1), p. 101, concludes that "Zosimus followed Eunapius more often than he deserted him."

[61] Zosimus, *HN* 2.43.1: "At this juncture, the Persians plundered the eastern cities, especially those in Mesopotamia. Although he was defeated in the war against them, Constantius nevertheless was determined to attack Magnentius and Vetranio and their armies."

[62] Zosimus, *HN* 3.8.1.

identification of Constantius as the real subject of Constantine's alleged Persian war, that the number of troops attributed to Constantine in this war, 20,000 men, better fits the early reign of Constantius II than it does that of Constantine. One does not have to believe Zosimus' claim that Constantine led 90,000 infantry against Maxentius in 312, or 120,000 infantry against Licinius c.316, in order to realise that he ought to have been able to field a far larger force than 20,000 men had he really decided upon a Persian expedition.[63] As the sole ruler of the empire, he ought to have been able to gather a force comparable to the 83,000 men whom Julian gathered for his Persian expedition in 363,[64] had he really contemplated such an expedition in the late 320s, say. On the contrary, Constantius II ruled only about a third of this empire until 340, and only about a half until 353. Hence his resources were always far more limited, and 20,000 men seems a good approximation of the size of force which he would have been able to field in the early 340s. This brings us back to the earlier question concerning the source of manpower for the *Persocomites* and its twin, the *equites Persae clibanarii*. Constantius may have attracted a few Persian deserters and adventurers to his side by 344, but far more significant is the fact that he had captured a sizeable Persian city only a few years earlier, and had deported its whole population to Thrace.[65] These unfortunate exiles would have constituted an excellent source of manpower for Constantius in his new enterprise. The men ought to have had some familiarity with the Persian use of *clibanarii* which he wished to imitate, and their loyalty could be relied upon because their families were effectively hostages for their good behaviour.

Finally, the Guidi-legend preserves another strange episode concerning Constantine which deserves some mention here also because it too refers to

---

[63] Zosimus, *HN* 2.15.1; 2.22.1. The *Origo Constantini* 5.16 preserves much more realistic figures when it states that Constantine led 20,000 men against Licinius' army of 35,000 in their first civil war c.316.

[64] Zosimus claims that Julian reviewed a force of 65,000 men at Circesium after he had already detached a diversionary force of 18,000 men (*HN* 3.12-13). Hence the total of 83,000 men. In so far as Libanius (*Or.* 18.214) and Ammianus (23.3.5) describe the diversionary force as consisting of 20,000 and 30,000 men respectively, Zosimus' figures seem reasonably accurate in this instance.

[65] Libanius, *Or.* 59.83-87. Libanius does not name the part of Thrace to which the Persians had been deported, but I shall argue elsewhere, on the basis of Malalas, *Chron.* 13.12, that they had probably been settled in and about Maximianopolis in Rhodope.

a Persian war, although it is a little less absurd than the account of Constantine's capture by the Persians and quite separate from it in the narrative.[66] Nevertheless, it may well represent the same process at work once more, the pasting of another excerpt from the same, or a similar, source into a pre-existing life of Constantine where the editor thought most appropriate. It purports to tell how the citizens of Byzantium put up a fierce resistance against Constantine following his defeat of Licinius in 324, and is of interest to us here because it claims that the Byzantines had hoped to defeat Constantine in a third and final engagement when he sent the bulk of his army back to garrison duty in Rome because of a Persian invasion there. Fortunately, Constantine saw a sign in the sky again just as he had in his war against Maxentius, remembered how helpful the sign had been on that occasion, and put it to use once more. He triumphed, of course, and captured Byzantium. Now, one hardly needs to emphasize that this tale is nonsense as it survives. The Persians did not attack the empire under Constantine, and they certainly never threatened Rome! But the tale of how an emperor finally triumphed in his third engagement with the enemy after witnessing a sign in the sky similar to that which had appeared in the sky before the defeat of Maxentius earlier, and this despite the fact that he was being threatened by the Persians also, is reminiscent of the circumstances in which Constantius II found himself in 351. He had suffered several defeats by the usurper Magnentius before he finally triumphed at Mursa, all in the same year that he had appointed his cousin Gallus as Caesar in the East in order to check the Persian threat there.[67] Most importantly, later sources attributed his victory at Mursa to the appearance in the sky of the same sign which had appeared to Constantine I before his victory over Maxentius in 312,[68] and Constantius seems to have encouraged contemporary commentators to compare his victory over Magnentius to that of his father

---

[66] Guidi (n. 3), 335-36; ch. 23 in the text as divided by Lieu and Montserrat (n. 7), pp. 126-27.

[67] See J. Šašel, 'The Struggle between Magnentius and Constantius II for Italy and Illyricum', *Ziva Antika* 21 (1971), pp. 205-16.

[68] Philostorgius, *HE* 3.26; *Chron. Pasch. s.a.* 351. Originally, the cross had only appeared in the sky above Jerusalem, and bishop Cyril of Jersusalem had written to Constantius reporting this phenomenon as a sign of divine favour towards him, but, as the above sources reveal, this distinction was soon lost, and tradition came to assert that Constantius and his men had themselves seen the cross over Jerusalem even though they were fighting Magnentius in far-away Pannonia.

over Maxentius.[69] In short, one suspects that one of the more important ingredients in the mix which gave rise to the present tale concerning Constantine's victory over the hostile Byzantines was a rather confused account of Constantius II's victory at Mursa in 351. Again, one suspects that confusion between the names of Constantine I and Constantius II played a key part in this process. The final text has a solid historical starting point in that Constantine had been forced to besiege Licinius in Byzantium for a short period in 324, although there is no evidence that the Byzantines continued the struggle after Licinius fled to Chalcedon.[70] But there was a link between Constantine's struggles against Licinius and Constantius' struggle against Magnentius in that Constantius had located his headquarters at Cibalae for a period in 351, in part because it reminded all that his father had defeated Licinius there (although in their first civil war in 316 rather than in their second in 324).[71] Hence there were several features of Constantius' campaign against Magnentius in 351 which may have contributed to its confused assimilation with events under Constantine I. Whatever the case, there is no intrinsic connection between the two episodes of Constantine's capture by the Persians and his defeat of the Byzantines at this stage in the Constantinian legend, even if such a connection does develop later, and the one argument need not explain both episodes.

To conclude, therefore, it is my argument that the story of Constantine I's Persian expedition resulting in his defeat, capture, but ultimate triumph, is a displaced and somewhat distorted account of the earliest phase of the war between Constantius II and Sapor II c.337-44. As for the *Persocomites* allegedly created as the result of this expedition, they are identifiable as the *comites* [*Persae*] *clibanarii* of the *Notitia Dignitatum*. This story most likely has its origin in a fragment from the lost history of Eunapius of Sardis which had been corrupted in its transmission. Its survival should be compared, perhaps, to that of an unusually detailed account of the deaths of Crispus and Fausta in another life of Constantine, the so-called Opitz-legend (*BHG* 365), whose origins may be traced back to Eunapius also, via

---

[69] Themistius, *Or.* 3.44b. See also D. Woods, 'A Persian at Rome: Ammianus and Eunapius, *Frg.* 68', in J.W. Drijvers and D. Hunt (eds.), *The Late Roman World and Its Historian: Interpreting Ammianus Marcellinus* (London, 1999), pp. 156-65.

[70] *Origo Constantini* 5.25-27; Zosimus, *HN* 2.23-24.

[71] Zosimus, *HN* 2.48.3.

Philostorgius.[72]

II   On the Identity of the Egyptian from Spain (Zosimus, *HN 2.29*)

In a famous passage the pagan historian Zosimus attributes the conversion of Constantine I to Christianity to the influence of an Egyptian from Iberia who persuaded him that baptism would purge him of his guilt for the killing of his wife and eldest son, Fausta and Crispus (*HN 2.29.3*):[73]

Αἰγύπτιός τις ἐξ Ἰβηρίας εἰς τὴν Ῥώμην ἐλθὼν καὶ ταῖς εἰς τὰ βασίλεια γυναιξὶν συνήθης γενόμενος, ἐντυχὼν τῷ Κωνσταντίνῳ πάσης ἁμαρτάδος ἀναιρετικὴν εἶναι τὴν τῶν Χριστιανῶν διεβεβαιώσατο δόξαν καὶ τοῦτο ἔχειν ἐπάγγελμα, τὸ τοὺς ἀσεβεῖς μεταλαμβάνοντας αὐτῆς πάσης ἁμαρτίας ἔξω παραχρῆμα καθίστασθαι.

A certain Egyptian, who had come from Spain to Rome and was intimate with the ladies of the court, met Constantine and assured him that the Christian religion was able to absolve him from guilt and that it promised every wicked man who was converted to it immediate release from all sin.[74]

The identity of this Egyptian is problematic, although his identification as bishop Ossius of Cordova (c.300-57) has long since won general acceptance.[75] The problem is that Ossius was of Spanish birth and origin, so it is difficult to understand why Zosimus should refer to him as an Egyptian. The most commonly accepted explanation is that it was a term of abuse,[76] although it is difficult to explain its exact connotations, since no

---

[72] See J. Bidez, 'Fragments nouveaux de Philostorge sur la vie de Constantin', *Byzantion* 10 (1935), pp. 403-37.

[73] For the background, see D. Woods, 'On the Death of the Empress Fausta', *G & R* 45 (1998), pp. 70-86.

[74] Trans. by R.T. Ridley, *Zosimus: New History* (Canberra, 1982), p. 37.

[75] For the history of this identification, see V.C. de Clerq, *Ossius of Cordova: A Contribution to the History of the Constantinian Period* (Washington, D.C. 1954), p. 53, n. 63. More recently, this identification has been accepted by, e.g. F. Paschoud, *Cinq Études sur Zosime* (Paris, 1975), pp. 40-43; D. Bowder *The Age of Constantine and Julian* (London, 1978), p. 33; Ridley (n. 74), p. 157; Lieu and Montserrat (n. 7), p. 17.

[76] E.g. A. Alföldi, *The Conversion of Constantine and Pagan Rome* (Oxford, 1948), p. 102, n. 1; J.H. Smith, *Constantine the Great* (New York, 1971), p. 213. Exceptionally, M. Grant, *The Emperor Constantine* (London, 1993), p. 141, accepts that Ossius really was

examples can be adduced to prove that it really was a term of abuse. For while it is true that, as a race, the Egyptians did enjoy a bad reputation as a contentious, bad-mannered, and superstitious people,[77] there is no evidence that contentious, bad-mannered or superstitious individuals were ever referred to as 'Egyptians' simply because of their possession of these qualities. Hence an alternative explanation has also been offered, that the description may have resulted from some misunderstanding concerning Ossius' trip to Alexandria in Egypt in 324.[78]

That this Egyptian from Iberia was a bishop seems assured by a parallel passage in the ecclesiastical history of Sozomen. He describes a pagan claim that, following the murder of his wife and son, Constantine had enquired of the philosopher Sopater concerning the means of his purification, and that when he had been told that this was not possible in this case, he had happened to meet some bishops who promised him that baptism would produce the required effect.[79] Hence his baptism. It is generally agreed that Sozomen's source in this matter is the *History* of Eunapius of Sardis, and that, since Zosimus simply condenses Eunapius' work for much of the earlier part of his history, Zosimus' Egyptian is probably identifiable as one of the anonymous bishops mentioned by Sozomen. The convincing recent argument that Zosimus actually combined two very different sources to produce his account of the conversion of Constantine, the *Actus Silvestri* as well as the *History* of Eunapius, does not change this.[80] The Egyptian from Iberia must be a bishop, and since Ossius of Cordova fulfils two of the three conditions, being both a bishop and Spanish, his identification as the bishop concerned has won widespread acceptance.

My concern here is that there is another bishop whose candidacy in this matter has as much to recommend it as that of Ossius. I refer here to bishop Paphnutius of Egypt. As I will demonstrate next, he also fulfils two of the three conditions, being both a bishop and Egyptian. So why should we prefer one candidate to the other in this matter? Before proceeding any further, it is important to emphasize that we are less concerned here with

---

of Egyptian birth.

[77] E.g. Amm. 22.6.1; Eunapius, *VS* 463; *SHA Quadrigae Tyrannorum* 8.5.

[78] See de Clerq (n. 75), p. 56.

[79] Sozomen, *HE* 1.5.

[80] See Fowden (n. 12), 146-70, at 163-65.

the status of the historical Paphnutius, whether he was really a bishop, whether he attended the council of Nicaea, or whether there was a historical Paphnutius even, than with the legend that had grown up about him by the end of the fourth century.[81] We are concerned here with the sort of information concerning this Paphnutius which was available to Eunapius, and the manner in which Zosimus adapted this, rather than with the historical accuracy of this information. The fact that, writing c.402, Rufinus of Aquileia already believed that Paphnutius had been a bishop suffices to prove that Eunapius probably thought so also, since they were contemporaries and Rufinus may be presumed to preserve information similar to that which would have been available to Eunapius. Hence when I refer to bishop Paphnutius of Egypt, I do not necessarily accept the existence of a bishop of this name under Constantine I, but refer only to the legendary figure as he existed by the end of the 4th-century.

Obviously, the first argument in favour of the identification of the legendary 'bishop' Paphnutius of Egypt with the mysterious Egyptian from Iberia must be that he was in fact Egyptian. Of the early church-historians, Rufinus refers to him as a 'bishop from the region of Egypt' (*episcopus ex Aegypti partibus*), Sozomen describes him as 'Paphnutius from Egypt' (Παφνούτιος ὁ ἐξ Αἰγύπτου), and Theodoret as 'Paphnutius the Egyptian' (Παφνούτιος ὁ Αἰγύπτιος).[82] Socrates is the most specific, describing him as 'Paphnutius from the Upper Thebais' (Παφνούτιος τε ὁ ἐκ τῆς ἄνω Θηβαΐδος) and as 'bishop of one of the cities of Upper Thebes' (μιᾶς πόλεως τῶν ἄνω Θηβῶν ἐπίσκοπος).[83] It is clear, therefore, that the name of Paphnutius' see dropped from the mainstream Christian historical tradition at an early date, if it had ever been present at all, so that he was known simply as 'the Egyptian', with the occasional acknowledgement that he actually came from the Upper Thebais.

A second point to consider must be his access to the imperial court and, more importantly, to Constantine himself. Rufinus describes his presence at the council of Nicaea in 325, and his relationship with the emperor, as

---

[81] See F. Winkelmann, 'Paphnutios, der Bekenner und Bischof', *Probleme der koptischen Literatur, I* (Halle, 1968), pp. 145-53.
[82] Rufinus, *HE* 10.4; Sozomen, *HE* 1.10; Theodoret, *HE* 1.6.
[83] Socrates, *HE* 1.8, 11.

follows (*HE* 10.4):

> There was also at the council the man of God bishop Paphnutius
> from Egypt, one of the confessors whom Maximian, after
> gouging out their right eyes and severing their left hams, had
> condemned to the mines. But there was in him such a grace of
> miracles that signs were worked through him no less than
> through the apostles of old. For he put demons to flight with a
> mere word and cured the sick by prayer alone. He is said to have
> returned sight to the blind and given back soundness of body to
> the crippled. Constantine regarded him with such veneration and
> love that many times he called him into the palace, embraced
> him, and bestowed fervent kisses on the eye which had been
> gouged out in his confession of faith.[84]

This is as strong as anything which survives concerning the relationship
between Constantine and Ossius. In his description of how Constantine sent
a letter to Alexandria in Egypt in 324 in an attempt to reconcile the two
sides in the growing Arian crisis there, Eusebius of Caesarea describes the
messenger as follows (*VC* 2.63):

> He forthwith selected from the Christians in his train one whom
> he knew to be approved for the sobriety and genuineness of his
> faith, and who before this time distinguished himself by the
> boldness of his religious profession, and sent him to negotiate
> peace between the dissentient parties at Alexandria.[85]

Eusebius' continuators rephrase his sentiments, and explicitly identify this
anonymous messenger with Ossius of Cordova, but do not preserve
anything which can be taken as proof that Constantine enjoyed a closer
relationship with Ossius than he did with any of the other bishops.[86] Indeed,
there are strong doubts whether they are right even to interpret these lines in
reference to Ossius.[87] Whatever the case, the real distinction between

---

[84] Trans. by P. Amidon, *The Church History of Rufinus of Aquileia: Books 10 and 11*
(New York, 1997), pp. 11-12.
[85] Trans. by E.C. Richardson, *NPNF* 1, 2nd Series (New York, 1890), p. 515.
[86] Socrates, *HE* 1.7; Sozomen, *HE* 1.16.
[87] B.H. Warmington, 'The Sources of Some Constantinian Documents in Eusebius'
Ecclesiastical History and Life of Constantine', in E. Livingstone (ed.), *Studia Patristica*

Constantine's relations with Ossius and Paphnutius lie in the official duties which he entrusted to the former.

The earliest explicit evidence for Ossius' association with Constantine occurs in a letter which Constantine sent to bishop Caecilian of Carthage in 313, which reveals that Constantine had requested Ossius to draw up a list of bishops in the diocese of Africa who deserved his financial support on account of the orthodoxy of their faith.[88] He also sent him to Alexandria in 324 with a letter for the parties in the Arian dispute there, as already noted, but the highlight of Ossius' career under Constantine was surely his appointment as president of the Council of Nicaea in 325. Yet these and other appointments prove little other than that Constantine regarded Ossius as a capable administrator, a tactful negotiator, and a good civil servant. They do not prove that the emperor relied on his advice more than that of any other bishop, nor that they enjoyed particularly good relations.[89] A number of different factors may have come into play here such as the education of the bishops from whom Constantine could choose for such tasks, their willingness to perform such tasks, or their physical ability even. In the case of Paphnutius, for example, the fact that his right eye had been gouged out, and his left-leg crippled, not to mention any other complications which may have resulted from his service in the mines, probably rendered him physically incapable of performing many of the tasks which fell to Ossius. If one wants to contrast the relative standing of these two individuals, whatever their clerical status, one should turn rather to the debate on celibacy which occurred at Nicaea, or rather was alleged to have occurred. According to our sources, Paphnutius spoke out boldly during the council against a proposal that clergy should refrain from intercourse with their wives after entering upon the priesthood.[90] In so far as

---

18 (Kalamazoo, 1989), pp. 93-97, argues that this description refers to the *notarius* Marianus, not Ossius, although T.G. Elliott, *The Christianity of Constantine the Great* (Scranton, 1996), p. 164, disagrees with him on the basis of Athanasius, *Apol. c. Arian.* 74.4 and 76.3.

[88] Eusebius, *HE* 10.6.1-3.

[89] In general, see B.H. Warmington, 'Did Constantine have "Religious Advisers" ?', in E. Livingstone (ed.), *Studia Patristica* 19 (Louvain, 1989), pp. 117-29.

[90] Socrates, *HE* 1.11; Sozomen, HE 1.23; Gelasius, *HE* 2.32. It is this, of course, which has attracted far more attention to Paphnutius than he might otherwise have received. See e.g. C. Cochini, *The Apostolic Origins of Priestly Celibacy* (San Francisco, 1990), pp. 195-200.

Ossius was president of the council, and had also attended the council of Elvira c.300 at which an identical proposal had already been passed, it has been argued that Ossius was the main force behind this proposal.[91] It was defeated, however, so on the one issue on which we can be sure that Ossius and Paphnutius did have strongly opposed views, Paphnutius' view triumphed. To be more precise, given the attempts by Constantine to impose a measure of uniformity in practice and doctrine on all the churches throughout the empire, Constantine allowed Paphnutius' view to triumph, i.e. he preferred Paphnutius' advice to that of Ossius, or so the tradition went by the end of the 4th-century.

It is appropriate at this point to consider the wider circumstances of Constantine's alleged conversation with the Egyptian from Iberia. When and where did it take place? If we are to believe Zosimus, then it took place at Rome, sometime after Constantine had gained sole control of the empire, and shortly after the deaths of Crispus and Fausta. At its face value, therefore, this seems to prove that this incident occurred during the summer of 326 when Constantine visited Rome for his vicennial celebrations.[92] But Zosimus' account of this incident cannot be taken at its face value because it is a composite formed from two different sources, Eunapius' *History* and the *Actus Silvestri*. Strictly speaking, in his initial account of Constantine's approach to Sopater seeking purification from his sin, Sozomen does not state where this encounter occurred. Nevertheless, he records later that the council of Nicaea sparked off a number of debates at Constantine's court between pagan philosophers and Christian bishops.[93] In one instance, a simple old man, highly esteemed as a confessor, but unskilled in logic, opposed a philosopher whom he managed to persuade to convert to Christianity, while on a second occasion bishop Alexander of Constantinople miraculously silenced his pagan opponent. Of particular interest to us here is Sozomen's claim that this second contest took place after Constantine had returned to Constantinople from Nicaea, i.e. during the winter of 325/6. It seems probable that Eunapius had included a pagan account of these same debates which took place during late 325 and early 326, and one wonders how he explained the success of the Christians. He could not deny their success, of course, since the subsequent history of

---

[91] See de Clerq (n. 75), p. 279.
[92] See Barnes (n. 11), p. 77.
[93] Sozomen, *HE* 1.18.

Constantine's reign put this beyond the shadow of a doubt, but he could hardly have brought himself to admit that the Christians genuinely got the better of the philosophers in the debates. The answer, I suggest, is that Eunapius explained the failure of Sopater and his fellow philosophers to persuade Constantine to return to traditional Roman beliefs on the basis that they had refused to offer him purification for his murders of his wife and son, but that the Christians had. So Sopater and his colleagues did not really lose the argument, since the Christians had cheated and seduced the emperor to their side by bribing him in effect.

It is my argument, therefore, that Eunapius located the debates between the pagan philosophers, who included Sopater, and the Christian bishops, who included the Egyptian from Iberia, at Constantinople rather than Rome, and during the spring of 326. Zosimus then changed the order of events slightly, so the debates were shifted to Rome during the summer of 326. This was how he resolved the conflict of evidence between Eunapius who set Constantine's conversion at Constantinople just before his last visit ever to Rome and the *Actus Silvestri* which set Constantine's baptism at Rome, not Constantinople. As far as we are presently concerned, the fact that these debates took place at Constantinople, not Rome, contributes little to the solution of the mystery concerning the identity of the Egyptian from Iberia, although we cannot now prefer to identify him as Ossius simply on the basis that Rome was in the West and he was a western bishop, whereas Paphnutius is not known ever to have left the East. The council of Nicaea left Paphnutius and Ossius both within a short distance of Constantinople in 325, and one does not doubt that such distinguished individuals were welcome in Constantine's entourage as he returned to his capital. Both were probably present during the debates of late 325 and early 326, and one may even suspect that the simple old confessor who persuaded a pagan philosopher to convert, according to Sozomen at least, was none other than Paphnutius.

In the final analysis, we know nothing concerning their wider careers under Constantine which enables us to distinguish which of Paphnutius or Ossius is to be preferred as the Egyptian from Iberia. We are back to the original problem. The description does not fit Ossius since he was not an Egyptian, while it does not fit Paphnutius since it is hardly likely that he ever visited Spain. On the face of things, we are seeking to identify an Egyptian bishop who travelled to Constantinople via Spain, an explanation for which route should tax even the best imagination. Rather than engage in ever more inventive interpretations of this phrase explaining why it does not really mean what it appears to say, let us question rather whether it is wise to accept this reading of the text as it stands. Two approaches suggest themselves.

On the one hand, one should remember that we depend for our knowledge of Zosimus' text on a single manuscript of the 11/12th-centuries, and that although late Byzantine sources may occasionally throw some indirect light on the correct readings on certain passages, this is not true in this case.[94] Furthermore, Zosimus' text contains mistakes whose very nature reveals that they are due to the faulty transmission of a text, whether of Eunapius' *History* as used by Zosimus, or of the source even which Eunapius himself had used. The best example is Zosimus' claim that the emperor Gratian was killed at Singidunum in Moesia, whereas he was actually killed at Lugdunum in Gaul.[95] At some point in the tradition, the first syllable of Lugdunum has been corrupted so that it was interpreted to read Singidunum instead, and the wider context developed accordingly. A similar occurrence may well lie at the heart of the present problem. Either Eunapius' copy of his original source text, or Zosimus' copy of Eunapius' *History*, contained a faulty reading which has gone unchallenged since. One of either the description of the Egyptian as an Egyptian or the description of his origin at Iberia before he arrived at Constantinople represents a faulty reading of the original text.

A second approach is possible also, though, and may well prove the more convincing. One notes that although his name is more correctly spelled 'Ossius', Greek sources render it as 'Hosius', doubtless because of its similarity to the Greek adjective ὅσιος 'holy'.[96] Athanasius of Alexandria, for example, enjoyed the play upon words contained in his name.[97] There is an obvious danger, therefore, that his name might be misinterpreted as a simple adjective rather than as a real name, particularly if one knows little about the church-history of the first half of the 4th-century. This is exactly

---

[94] See F. Paschoud, *Zosime. Histoire Nouvelle: Tome I (Livres I et II)* (Paris, 1971), pp. LXXV-LXXXVIII.
[95] Zosimus, *HN* 4.35.6. Cf. Socrates, *HE* 5.11.
[96] See de Clerq (n. 75), pp. 44-48.
[97] Athanasius, *Apol. de Fuga* 5; *Hist. Arian.* 45.

what has happened in this case, I suggest. Eunapius' source named the two bishops Paphnutius the Egyptian and Osius from Spain in close sequence, but Eunapius misinterpreted the name Osius as the adjective 'holy' in continued reference to Paphnutius the Egyptian, and so reached the mistaken conclusion that the 'holy' Egyptian had come from Spain, or Iberia as he preferred to call it in accordance with his classicizing style. Naturally, he could not accept the description of a Christian bishop as 'holy', and so omitted it altogether.

In conclusion, Eunapius described a series of debates between pagan philosophers and Christian bishops at the court of Constantine I during late 325 and early 326, and explained the success of the Christians by claiming that they had seduced Constantine to their cause by offering him purification for his murder of his wife and eldest son. He named the leader of the philosophers as Sopater, and the leader of the bishops as Paphnutius the Egyptian who had come from Iberia. Unfortunately, his description of the leader of the bishops resulted from his misinterpretation of the first two names of a longer list of bishops. He misinterpreted the name of one bishop, Hosius from Spain, as an adjective 'holy' in reference to a second bishop, Paphnutius from Egypt, to reach the understanding that the Egyptian Paphnutius had travelled to Constantine's court at Constantinople from Spain. Later, when Zosimus was summarizing Eunapius' *History* for his own work, he decided to leave Paphnutius anonymous, referring to him simply as a certain Egyptian, and in order to reconcile Eunapius' account of Constantine's conversion with the account of his baptism in the *Actus Silvestri*, he transferred the alleged conversion to Rome instead.

III   The Burning of a *Hadrianeum* under Jovian

That volume of the *Excerpta Historica* known as the *Excerpta de Virtutibus et Vitiis (EV)* has preserved a condensed account of the reign of the emperor Jovian (363-4) so similar to that found in the *Suda* that it is clear that they depend on the same ultimate source. This was probably Eunapius' *History*, or so it is agreed. One notes, however, that each account is two steps removed from Eunapius' original. For the *EV* attributes its account to the 7th-century historian John of Antioch, and although the *Suda* does not attribute its account to any author in particular, the fact that it begins with the false claim that Jovian had resigned from the army under the emperor Julian rather than offer sacrifice suggests that it derives from a Christian

116

intermediary source.[98] These accounts tell us relatively little about Jovian which we do not know from other sources already, with one notable exception. Both claim that Jovian was responsible for the burning of a temple built by the emperor Hadrian.

Καθαπτόμενοι καὶ τῆς γυναικὸς αὐτοῦ διὰ τὴν τοῦ ἱεροῦ καταστροφήν. Ἀδριανὸς μὲν γὰρ ὁ βασιλεὺς εἰς ἀποθέωσιν καὶ τιμὴν τοῦ πατρὸς Τραϊανου ἔκτισε μικρόν τινα καὶ χαριέστατον ναὸν, ὃν Ἰουλιανὸς ὁ παραβάτης βιβλιοθήκην κατεσκεύασεν· ὃν σὺν τοῖς βιβλίοις Ἰοβιανος κατέκαυσε (Exc. de Virt. 63).[99]

They [the Antiochenes] also blamed his wife for the destruction of the temple. For the emperor Hadrian built for the worship and honour of his father Trajan a most beautiful, small temple, which the apostate Julian made into a library. This Jovian burned with its books.

ὁ δὲ Ἰοβιανός, ἐκ τῆς γυναικὸς αὐτοῦ κινηθεὶς τὸν ὑπὸ Ἀδριανοῦ τοῦ βασιλέως κτισθέντα ναὸν χαριέστατον ἐς ἀποθέωσιν τοῦ πατρὸς Τραϊανου, παρὰ δὲ τοῦ Ἰουλιανοῦ κατασταθέντα βιβλιοθήκην εὐνούχῳ τινὶ Θεοφίλῳ, κατέφλεξε σὺν πᾶσιν οἷς εἶχε βιβλίοις, αὐτῶν τῶν παλλακίδων ὑφαπτουσῶν μετὰ γέλωτος τὴν πυράν (Suda I 401).[100]

Urged by his wife, Jovian burned the most beautiful temple built by the emperor Hadrian for the worship of his father Trajan which had been turned into a library by the eunuch Theophilus at the command of Julian, together with all the books which it held, and his concubines set the fire with laughter.

---

[98] In general, see Banchich (n. 1), pp. 39-57. Given the differences between the two accounts, it does not seem possible that the Suda's account of the burning of the temple is derived from the excerpt of John of Antioch as preserved in the EV.

[99] Exc. de Virt. 63 = John of Antioch, frag. 181 in Müller (n. 42), p. 607.

[100] Suda I 401 = Eunapius, frag. 29.1 in Blockley (n. 1), p. 46.

This is an important claim as far as Jovian's religious policy is concerned, since it seems to reveal him as an active persecutor of paganism. Yet it is a controversial claim, not least because other evidence suggests that Jovian exercised a policy of toleration.[101] Ammianus Marcellinus records that animals were sacrificed for Jovian immediately after his accession, while Libanius claims that sacrifices had been allowed to continue from the reign of Julian until that of Jovian's successors, the brothers Valentinian I and Valens.[102] Moreover, as the head of an embassy from the Senate of Constantinople, Themistius had delivered a panegyric before Jovian at Ancyra on 1 January 364 in which he had praised him for his religious toleration and argued for the continuation or extension of this policy.[103] Eunapius himself admits that Jovian had continued to honour two of the more notorious of Julian's religious advisors, Maximus and Priscus.[104] It is generally agreed, therefore, that whatever his long term intentions may have been, Jovian was not yet secure enough on the throne by his death on 17 February 364 to have begun an active persecution of pagans. So what had happened to the temple built by Hadrian?

The claim by the *Suda* that Jovian had been inspired by his wife to burn the temple, and that his concubines had laughed as they set it on fire, is clearly ridiculous. It is reminiscent of the claim that the courtesan Thais had persuaded a drunken Alexander the Great to allow her, together with the other courtesans present at the feast, to lead the burning of the great palace of the Persian kings at Persepolis in 330 BC.[105] Given that Alexander had continued to be a popular choice for late antique authors when they wished

---

[101] So, for example, N. Lenski, *Valens and the Fourth Century Empire* (doctoral dissertation submitted at Princeton University, 1995: UMI no. 9605072), p. 17, accepts the burning of the temple at Antioch but attributes responsibility to rioters rather than to the emperor. He compares this incident to the destruction of the estates of a certain Datianus following the arrival at Antioch of the news of the death of Jovian himself (Libanius, *Epp.* 1184-86).

[102] Amm. 25.6.1; Libanius, *Or.* 30.7.

[103] See J. Vanderspoel, *Themistius and the Imperial Court: Oratory, Civic Duty, and Paideia from Constantius to Theodosius* (Ann Arbor, 1995), pp. 148-53.

[104] Eunapius, *VS* 7.4.10, 478.

[105] Curtius 5.7.1-7; Diodorus 17.72.1-6; Plutarch, *Alex.* 38. See N.G.L. Hammond, 'The Archaeological and Literary Evidence for the Burning of the Persepolis Palace', *CQ* 42 (1992), pp. 358-64.

to draw historical parallels,[106] and that Jovian does seem to have indulged too much in wine and women,[107] one suspects that it is some such parallel which lies at the heart of present problem. We know little about Jovian's wife Charito other than her name and the fact that she was the daughter of a senior military commander of Pannonian origin,[108] and it may be that she encouraged her husband to forgive those responsible for the burning of the temple after the event. It would be anachronistic in the extreme, however, to view her as an active supporter of the destruction of temples in the manner, for example, that the empress Eudoxia was to support the destruction of the temples at Gaza in 402.[109] At best, the authors of the *EV* and the *Suda*, or of their sources rather, have each misunderstood a parallel between the irresponsible behaviour of Jovian and that of Alexander, both of whom indulged too much in wine and women, so that they reached the mistaken conclusion that his concubines had accompanied Jovian as he set the temple on fire, just as Thais and her fellow courtesans had accompanied Alexander as he set fire to the palace at Persepolis. But did Jovian really set the temple on fire? I do not doubt that this is what Eunapius originally said, that Jovian burned a temple built by Hadrian, but Eunapius was bitterly anti-Christian and may have blamed Jovian for something for which he bore little or no real responsibility.[110] Hence when Eunapius claimed that Jovian burned a temple, he may have meant no more than that Jovian was responsible for ordering, or allowing, a temple to be burned, which claim was entirely false, and not that he was personally present at the burning itself. But our epitomators did not notice this, and misled by the parallel between Jovian and Alexander, concluded that Jovian must have been present at the burning of the temple just as Alexander had been present at the burning of the palace.

The realisation that Jovian need not have been present at the burning of the temple for Eunapius to have held him responsible still, frees one to consider a wide range of possible locations for this incident. A much longer description of the reception of Jovian at Antioch, followed by an account of

---

[106] For examples, see R.J. Lane Fox, 'The Itinerary of Alexander: Constantius to Julian', *CQ* 47 (1997), pp. 239-52.
[107] Amm. 25.10.15.
[108] Zonaras, *Ann.* 13.14; Amm. 25.8.9.
[109] On this incident, see F.R. Trombley, *Hellenic Religion and Christianization c.370-529* I (Leiden, 1993), pp. 207-22.
[110] Photius, *Bibl. Cod.* 77.

his actions while there, including a claim that he burned a temple of Hadrian, i.e. that he gave the orders, or allowed, a temple to be burned, has been so abbreviated as to give the impression that this temple was itself in Antioch. But this was not necessarily the case. In fact, the wider evidence points to the location of this temple at Alexandria in Egypt instead.

Firstly, Alexandria was notorious for its inter-communal strife which often resulted in the occupation or destruction of a rival place of worship.[111] For example, the Arian bishop George of Alexandria had destroyed a *Mithraeum* when preparing a site for the construction or extension of a church in the precinct of the *Caesareum* in late 361, and it was his treatment of the materials discovered in this *Mithraeum* more than anything which so enraged the pagan mob.[112] He was particularly unfortunate in that the news of the death of his imperial patron Constantius II reached Alexandria only days later, so that he was jailed first before a mob stormed the jail and killed him almost a month later on 24 December 361. Again, a pagan mob burned down the main church at this site, which the Christians referred to as 'the church called the *Caesareum*', on 21 July 366, although the immediate cause of this riot remains unknown.[113] This is in stark contrast to Antioch where such religious strife was almost unheard of. For while it is true that the famous temple of Apollo at Daphne in the suburbs of Antioch was burned to the ground in 362, this was not the result of mob-violence.[114] Indeed, it did not prove possible to blame any individual Christian even for this disaster, and the pagan Ammianus goes so far as to admit that the fire may have been started accidentally. It is noteworthy also that Julian responded by closing the Great Church at Antioch, not by destroying it. In brief, Antioch had not experienced the same level of religious violence as Alexandria, so that it is difficult to explain why this event should have

---

[111] See C. Haas, *Alexandria in Late Antiquity: Topography and Social Conflict* (Baltimore, 1997), esp. pp. 278-330.

[112] Only Socrates, *HE* 3.2, followed by Sozomen, *HE* 5.7, mentions the *Mithraeum*, although Amm. 22.11.9 and *Hist. Aceph.* 2.10 confirm the construction work. In general, see A. Martin, 'Les premiers siècles du christianisme à Alexandrie. Essai de topographie religieuse (IIIe-IVe siècles)', *REA* 30 (1984), 211-25. On the circumstances of this incident, generally misundertood, see D. Woods, 'The Final Commission of Artemius the Former *Dux Aegypti*', *BMGS* 23 (1999), pp. 2-24.

[113] *Festal Index* 38. Barnes (n. 48), p. 163, tentatively suggests that the correct date may be 21 July 365 when a huge tidal wave caused massive destruction throughout the eastern Mediterranean.

[114] E.g. Amm. 22.13.1-3; John Chrysostom, *de S. Babyla* 93-109 (Schatkin).

occurred there in particular. Nor is it credible that anyone would have dared to commit such an outrage while the emperor was present in the city, since this would have been interpreted as a direct challenge to his authority, and have been dealt with accordingly. So one suspects that this incident actually occurred at Alexandria, probably shortly after the arrival there on 19 August 363 of the news of the death of Julian.[115] It should best be compared to the riots which led to the murder of bishop George shortly after the Alexandrians had learned of the death of Constantius. Some seem to have drawn the wrong conclusion from Julian's failure earlier to punish the city as a whole for this murder, and to have decided that the administrative indecision consequent upon the change of régime again presented them with another opportunity once more for riotous behaviour.

Next, an inscription dated 170 attests the existence of a *Hadrianeum* in Alexandria, which must seem a strong candidate for identification with our temple which was built by Hadrian in honour of Trajan.[116] In so far as it has been argued that the *Hadrianeum* was situated in the vicinity of the *Caesareum*, then it would have been suitably close to that flashpoint for other riots at this period to have become increasingly endangered itself also.[117] Indeed, there is no evidence that Hadrian built a temple of Trajan at Antioch other than the passage under discussion here.[118] It is particularly noteworthy that the Antiochene John Malalas does not mention it among the long list of other projects at Antioch whose construction he attributes to Hadrian.[119]

Thirdly, the claim by the *Suda* that Julian had instructed a eunuch called Theophilus to make the *Hadrianeum* into a library suggests the identification of this Theophilus with the Theophilus mentioned by Julian in a letter to the *praefectus Aegypti* Ecdicius.[120] Julian wrote to Ecdicius to inform him of the height of the Nile on 20 September 362, and mentioned that he had learned this from the στρατοπεδάρχης Theophilus, by which he seems to mean that Theophilus was the *dux Aegypti* at this time. This is

---

[115] *Hist. Aceph.* 4.1.

[116] *IGRR* I. 1060.

[117] A. Adriani, *Repertorio d'arte dell'Egitto greco-roman* (Palermo, 1966), pp. 222-23.

[118] A.R. Birley, *Hadrian: The Restless Emperor* (London, 1997), p. 153, follows the standard interpretation of this passage in locating the temple at Antioch.

[119] Malalas, *Chron.* 11.14.

[120] Julian, *Ep.* 45 (Wright).

not to claim that the *dux Aegypti* Theophilus really was a eunuch. His description as such belongs to the author of the *Suda*, or his intermediary source, rather than to Eunapius. One should compare his role in the construction of a library at the *Hadrianeum* to the role of the *dux Aegypti* Diodorus in the construction work on or near the *Mithraeum* in late 361. They merely provided the security for these projects in a highly volatile section of the city.

Next, it is an interesting coincidence both that Julian ordered the construction of a library in the *Hadrianeum* and that he was very concerned also to recover the library which had used to belong to the murdered bishop George. Two letters attest his interest in George's library, the first to the *praefectus Aegypti* Ecdicius, and the second to an otherwise unknown Porphyrius who may be tentatively identified as George's former *notarius*.[121] In his letter to Ecdicius, Julian said that he wanted the Christian writings within George's library to be destroyed, but that this should be done only after all the books had been safely recovered, in order to ensure that none of the non-Christian works were destroyed also. Then, in his letter to Porphyrius, he specified that all the books were to be sent to him at Antioch. But we do not know that the books were ever actually sent to him there. His letter to Porphyrius must postdate his arrival at Antioch in July 362, and if his threats are any guide in this matter, it would seem that he was not very pleased at the progress made to date in tracing all of George's books. It is possible, therefore, that the library in the *Hadrianeum* was not intended as a permanent institution but was a temporary repository for George's books until his whole library had been recovered once more and was finally ready to be sent on to Julian. One notes, for example, that despite Zosimus' claim that Julian built a library at Constantinople where he then deposited all his books, a speech which Themistius delivered in the eastern Senate in 357 proves that it was really Constantius who had founded this library.[122] The most that one can claim for Julian is that he had added to its collection. So the claim that Julian ordered the creation of a library in the *Hadrianeum* may represent a similar exaggeration of a more mundane reality, that the *Hadrianeum* had served as a temporary storage depot for the collection and re-cataloguing of George's library.

---

[121] Julian, *Ep.* 24; *Ep.* 38 (Wright).
[122] Zosimus, *HN* 3.11.3; Themistius, *Or.* 4.59d-60a.

Finally, it should be noted that a number of pieces of circumstantial evidence combine to suggest that Eunapius had visited Alexandria and had probably witnessed first-hand the destruction of the *Serapeum* there in 391. This would explain both his knowledge of and interest in earlier acts of violence against the temples there, and why it is that he records an event which has passed unattested otherwise.

It is my argument, therefore, that the original description of Jovian's reign by Eunapius has been seriously distorted by successive epitomators. A simple parallel between the characters of Jovian and Alexander the Great was extended beyond Eunapius' original intent to include his description of Jovian's responsibility, as he saw it, for the burning of a temple built by Hadrian. The same epitomators merely assumed from the context that the temple in question was at Antioch, whereas this was simply the location of Jovian when he happened to receive the news about the burning of the temple in Alexandria. Jovian did not burn down a temple which the emperor Hadrian had built at Antioch, and which a eunuch by the name of Theophilus had converted into a library under Julian. Rather, a Christian mob burned down the *Hadrianeum* at Alexandria which was under the protection of the *dux Aegypti* Theophilus shortly after they had learned the good news of Jovian's accession.

IV   Goths or Monks?

In his *Lives of the Sophists*, Eunapius preserves the strange allegation that monks had assisted the Goth Alaric during his invasion of Greece in 396. They had apparently opened the pass of Thermopylae to him (*VS* 7.3.5, 476):

> ὅτε Ἀλλάριχος ἔχων τοὺς βαρβάρους διὰ τῶν Πυλῶν
> παρῆλθεν, ὥσπερ διὰ σταδίου καὶ ἱπποκρότου πεδίου
> τρέχων· τοιαύτας αὐτῷ τὰς πύλας ἀπέδειξε τῆς
> Ἑλλάδος ἥ τε τῶν τὰ φαιὰ ἱμάτια ἐχόντων ἀκωλύτως
> προσπαρεισελθόντων ἀσέβεια, καὶ ὁ τῶν ἱεροφαντικῶν
> θεσμῶν παραρραγεὶς νόμος καὶ σύνδεσμος.

> [It was the time] when Alaric with his barbarians invaded Greece by the pass of Thermopylae, as easily as though he were

123

traversing an open stadium or a plain suitable for cavalry. For this gateway of Greece was thrown open to him by the impiety of the men clad in black raiment, who entered Greece unhindered along with him, and by the fact that the laws and restrictions of the hierophantic ordinances had been rescinded.[123]

While it is true that he does not actually refer to the monks as such (μοναχοί), it is commonly accepted that this is what he means here by 'the men clad in black raiment.'[124] So, for example, he follows his specific statement that monks assisted in the destruction of the *Serapeum* at Alexandria in 391 with the explanation that every man who wore a black cloak and wanted to behave in unseemly fashion in public possessed the power of a tyrant.[125] Their black dress was most distinctive, and served to emphasize their rejection of the conventional values of late antique society, so pagans tended to refer to monks in derisive fashion as 'men-in-black'. For example, in a speech which he delivered in his defence c.380, Libanius described monks as men who were restrained only as far as their dress was concerned.[126] Similarly, in his speech on behalf of pagan temples which he addressed to the emperor Theodosius I himself in 390, Libanius described them as the 'men-in-black' who ate more than elephants.[127] There is no reason to doubt, therefore, that Eunapius really does mean us to understand that monks assisted Alaric in his invasion of Greece.

Several problems now present themselves. First, why should monks have wanted to assist Alaric? True, he was an Arian Christian, but this does not suffice to explain their action.[128] One immediately calls to mind that fragment of Eunapius' *History* in which he claims that the Goths had used false bishops to deceive the emperors into allowing them to enter the empire, and that these had been accompanied by monks also:

---

[123] Text and translation from W.C. Wright (ed.), *Philostratus and Eunapius: Lives of the Sophists* (Loeb Classical Library 134: Cambridge, Mass. 1921), p. 438.

[124] E.g. Wright (n. 123), p. 438; Blockley (n. 59), p. 18; R.J. Penella, *Greek Philosophers and Sophists in the Fourth Century AD: Studies in Eunapius of Sardis* (Leeds, 1990), p. 143.

[125] Eunapius, *VS* 6.11.7, 472: μέλαιναν φορῶν ἐσθῆτα.

[126] Libanius, *Or.* 2.32.

[127] Libanius, *Or.* 30.8: μελανειμονοῦντες

[128] Augustine, *Civ. Dei* 1.2; Orosius, *Adv. Pag.* 7.37.2.

ἦν δέ τι καὶ τῶν καλουμένων μοναχῶν παρ' αὐτοῖς γένος, κατὰ μίμησιν τῶν παρὰ τοῖς πολεμίοις ἐπιτετηδευμένον, οὐδὲν ἐχούσης τῆς μιμήσεως πραγματῶδες καὶ δύσκολον, ἀλλὰ ἐξῆρκει φαιὰ ἱμάτια σύρουσι καὶ χιτώνια πονηροῖς τε εἶναι καὶ πιστεύεσθαι.

They also had with them some of the tribe of so-called 'monks', whom they had decked out in imitation of the monks amidst their enemies. The imitation was neither laborious nor difficult, but it sufficed for them to trail along grey cloaks and tunics to both become and be accepted as evil-doers.[129]

This passage had traditionally been interpreted to refer to events under Theodosius I, but it has recently been proven that it really refers to the Gothic crossing of the Danube in 376.[130] It would appear, therefore, that the Goths had brought their own monks with them into the empire as early as 376, and the obvious suggestion is that it was Gothic monks also who opened the pass of Thermopylae to Alaric in 396. Yet while this may well explain the apparent sympathy of the monks towards Alaric, it does not explain how they were able to accomplish their aim.

This is our second problem. How did monks, Gothic or otherwise, come to be able to betray the pass of Thermopylae to Alaric? While some Roman officers may well have been lulled into a false sense of security by the false oaths of false bishops back in 376, exactly as Eunapius alleges, such tricks were hardly still effective by 396. So while it is all very well to make vague assertions to the effect that it was the monks who betrayed Thermopylae to Alaric in 396, it is difficult to understand how they could have achieved this in practice. This assumes, of course, that there really was a garrison at Thermopylae at this time, and that Eunapius does not mean that some monks merely directed Alaric towards this pass, guarded or not. Furthermore, the vague nature of his claim, that it was the impiety of the monks which delivered Thermopylae to Alaric, might even encourage one

---

[129] *Exc. de Sent.* 53 = Eunapius, *frag.* 48.2 in Blockley (n. 1), pp. 76-77.

[130] See P. Heather, 'The Crossing of the Danube and the Gothic Conversion', *GRBS* 27 (1986), pp. 289-318, at 305-10, followed by N. Lenski, 'The Gothic Civil War and the Date of the Gothic Conversion', *GRBS* 36 (1995), 51-87, at 70-71. Both accept Eunapius at face-value, that some Goths really did disguise themselves as Roman monks in order to gain passage into the empire.

to suspect that the connection between their alleged impiety and Alaric's invasion is a matter of personal interpretation only, since this is clearly true of the other cause which Eunapius adduces for the success of this invasion, that "the laws and restrictions of the hierophantic ordinances had been rescinded." Nevertheless, his statement that the monks entered Greece alongside Alaric suggests that Eunapius really did think that there were monks physically present with Alaric at Thermopylae in 396, just as they had been present with the Goths crossing the Danube in 376.

This brings us to a third problem. How do we reconcile Eunapius' account of Alaric's success at Thermopylae with that preserved by Zosimus? According to Zosimus, Alaric secretly sent to Gerontius, the commander of the garrison at Thermopylae, in order to announce his coming.[131] Gerontius then withdrew with his guards, and allowed Alaric to enter Greece unhindered. But where do the monks fit into this version of events?[132] Opinions differ. The problem is that although it is generally agreed that Zosimus did little more than summarize Eunapius' *History* for most of his account of the 4th-century, there are important exceptions which point to his occasional use of other sources also.[133] Is this another exception? We cannot be sure on the present evidence, since the apparent differences between the two accounts may well be explicable in terms of their different contexts, and the different aims of Eunapius in his *History* and his *Lives of the Sophists*.[134] So Eunapius may well have believed that some monks really did play a part in the larger scheme of events which saw Gerontius withdraw from Thermopylae in the face of Alaric's advance, but this only brings us back to the previous problem. How could monks have played any serious part in persuading Gerontius to abandon Thermopylae?

---

[131] Zosimus, *HN* 5.5.5-6.
[132] W.J. Cherf, 'The Thermopylae Garrison of *Vita Claudii* 16', *CPh* 88 (1993), pp. 230-36, argues that, writing c.397, the anonymous author of the notorious *Historia Augusta* based a fictitious event in the life of the emperor Claudius Gothicus (268-70) on events at Thermopylae in 396, but there is nothing to hint that he knew of the alleged involvement of monks in the events of 396.
[133] E.g. P. Heather, *Goths and Romans 332-489* (Oxford, 1991), pp. 147-48, argues that Zosimus has inserted a confused summary of the Gothic war of 376-82 from a second source into his basic Eunapian account.
[134] See F. Paschoud, *Zosime. Histoire Nouvelle. Tome III, 1re partie (Livre 5)* (Paris, 1986), pp. 91-94.

The abandonment of Thermopylae by Gerontius in the face of Alaric is a serious problem, whether or not we accept that monks played any part in this. Our sources for the events of 395-6 are all hostile towards Alaric, and depict him as a barbarian rebel who ravaged Greece. Hence the traditional interpretation of Alaric as a hostile invader,[135] which requires either that Gerontius was a traitor acting in collusion with Alaric, or that he was forced to withdraw because of some military weakness. It has also been argued, though, that Alaric was actually operating on behalf of the Eastern government at Constantinople, as the *magister militum per Illyricum*, and had been sent to Greece in order to prevent Stilicho repossessing it for the West.[136] According to this interpretation, Gerontius opened Thermopylae to Alaric because he had been instructed to do so by his government. As far as we are presently concerned, however, it remains difficult to understand how monks were involved in this process, whether Gerontius withdrew because he was in collusion with Alaric, because of some military weakness, or because he had been ordered to do so.

So what really happened at Thermopylae in 396? It is possible, of course, that Eunapius lied, that he simply invented his tale concerning Alaric and the monks in order to depict Christians in the worst possible light once more. It was a favourite accusation of pagan polemicists that Christians could not be trusted to defend the empire, while Christians were extremely proud to be able to point to evidence to the contrary. One may contrast Christian pride in the role which bishop Jacob of Nisibis played in the defence of his city against the Persians in 336,[137] to pagan rumours that bishop Heliodorus of Bezabde had betrayed his city to the Persians in 360.[138] Similarly, the pagan historian Ammianus Marcellinus draws repeated attention to the role of Christian clergy as the ambassadors of Rome's enemies.[139] There is no evidence, however, that Eunapius would have deliberately lied in this matter, not least because such a lie would have been counter-productive anyway. There would have been no point to a claim which any interested Christian could easily have refuted. Hence I do

---

[135] See A. Cameron, *Claudian: Poetry and Propaganda at the Court of Honorius* (Oxford, 1970), pp. 168-76; Heather (n. 133), pp. 199-204.
[136] See T.S. Burns, *Barbarians within the Gates of Rome: A Study of Roman Military Policy and the Barbarians, ca. 375-425 AD* (Bloomington, 1994), pp. 165-67.
[137] E.g. Jerome, *Chron. s.a.* 338; Philostorgius, *HE* 3.23; Theodoret, *HE* 2.30.1-14.
[138] Amm. 20.7.7-9.
[139] Amm. 29.5.15, 31.12.8, 31.15.6.

not doubt that Eunapius genuinely believed that monks really did help Alaric at Thermopylae. The real question is whether he was right to believe this.

It is my argument that Eunapius was so blinded by his hate for Christians in general, and for monks in particular, that he seriously misinterpreted his source(s) both for the Gothic crossing of the Danube in 376 and for Alaric's invasion of Greece in 396. On each occasion he misinterpreted a classicizing Greek term for one of the newly-arrived tribes from across the Danube in reference to Christian monks instead. In brief, he mistook references to a tribe known as the 'Blackcloaks' (Μελάγχλαινοι) as a variation on the common pagan disparagement of monks as the 'men-in-black', much because it appealed to his prejudice that Christians were always to be found hand-in-hand with Rome's enemies.

Herodotus had identified the 'Blackcloaks' as a trans-Danubian tribe that lived north of the Royal Scythians, but he had also emphasized that they were not themselves Scythian.[140] Writing c.AD 101, however, Dio Chrysostom left us a brief description of the inhabitants of Borysthenes in which he claimed that they each wore a small black cloak, and that most of their clothing was black in fact, as a result of the influence of a certain tribe of Scythians, the 'Blackcloaks'.[141] Of later writers, Ammianus twice mentions the 'Blackcloaks', or *Melanchlaenae* as he calls them, but does so in his scientific digressions, and does not attempt to label any of the recent migrant groups within the empire as *Melanchlaenae*.[142] Procopius proves little more helpful. For while he clearly identifies the 'Blackcloaks' as a Scythian people, he does not attempt to pin this label on any contemporary group in particular.[143] Hence by late antiquity the general consensus seems to have been that the 'Blackcloaks' were a Scythian people, but since classicizing historians tended to refer to all trans-Danubian groups as Scythians, this does not help us to determine whether this label had become attached to any particular group, Gothic or not.

---

[140] Herodotus 4.20.
[141] Dio Chrysostom, *Or.* 36.7.
[142] Amm. 22.8.31, 31.2.15.
[143] E.g. Procopius, *Bella* 3.2.2, 8.5.6.

I argue, therefore, that when the Goths crossed the Danube in 376, they did not bring any monks with them, real or otherwise, not as far as the present evidence is concerned at least. Rather, they included within their number a group whom Eunapius' source identified as 'Blackcloaks', and whom Eunapius proceeded to misidentify as monks. He then proceeded to complicate things further by denying that they had been real Roman monks at all, but had only been disguised as such in order to deceive the Romans. Three arguments may be adduced in favour of this hypothesis. First, the fact that Eunapius should refer to the monks as a 'tribe' (γένος) is significant since it suggests that this term was present in his source also, and reminds one of Dio Chrysostom's description of the 'Blackcloaks' as a 'tribe of Scythians' (γένος Σκυθῶν). It is not a natural term to use of a group of monks. So Eunapius' reference to a 'tribe of so-called "monks"' originated as a reference to a 'tribe of so-called "Blackcloaks"', one suspects. Indeed, it may have been the use of this term by his source which had encouraged Eunapius in his misinterpretation of the name of the 'Blackcloaks' in the first place. For the term 'tribe' can have a pejorative sense in Greek (either γένος or ἔθνος), much as in modern English, and one depends on the context to determine whether any particular use is pejorative or not. Fragments of Eunapius preserve his dismissive references to 'the tribe of villains and criminals' and 'the tribe of eunuchs', so that it does not surprise that he should have misinterpreted a technical use of the term 'tribe' (γένος) on this occasion in a pejorative sense.[144]

Next, it is difficult to understand what was so different about the alleged Gothic monks that they had to be disguised in order to make them look like the monks among their enemies, i.e. Roman monks. After all, Christianity, including monasticism, had been introduced among the Goths by Roman citizens.[145] We know, for example, that the heretical bishop Audius of Mesoptamia had sent missionaries into Gothic territory when exiled to the neighbouring Roman province of Scythia under the emperor Constantius II,

---

[144] *Suda* I 437 = Eunapius, *frag.* 25.1 in Blockley (n. 1), p. 37: τὸ τῶν πονηρῶν ἔθνος καὶ ἀδικούντων; *Suda* Σ 897 = Eunapius, *frag.* 65.7 in Blockley (n. 1), p. 99: τὸ τῶν εὐνούχων ἔθνος. The poet Claudian is similarly dismissive of the 'tribe' (*genus*) of eunuchs: *In Eutropium* I.332, 415.
[145] See R.W. Mathisen, 'Barbarian Bishops and the Churches "in barbaricis gentibus" during Late Antiquity', *Speculum* 72 (1997), pp. 664-97.

and that these had founded monasteries.[146] Strictly speaking, therefore, both groups of monks from either side of the Danube, Gothic or Roman, ought to have looked pretty much indistinguishable, especially since they had probably remained in almost continuous contact with one another. One recalls Ambrose of Milan's famous attack upon Iulianus Valens, bishop of Poetovio, because he dared to wear neck- and arm-bands in the manner of the Goths,[147] and admits that Gothic monks may also have adapted their dress somewhat in the light of local Gothic custom, but it remains hard to credit that their ordinary appearance differed from that of Roman monks to the extent that Eunapius requires. Hence Eunapius' misinterpretation of his source has forced him to assume that there were two very different types of monk, Gothic and Roman, the absurdity of which does not seem to have struck Eunapius himself, since he regarded all monasticism as absurd anyway.

Finally, had monks been as numerous among the Goths at this period as Eunapius would have us believe, then Ammianus ought to have mentioned them also in his detailed account of their entrance into the empire which culminated at the battle of Adrianopolis in 378. He does mention that the Gothic chief Fritigern sent a Christian priest as an envoy to the emperor Valens shortly before this battle, and that the victorious Goths sent a Christian, probably a priest also, to deliver their demand for the surrender of Adrianopolis itself after the battle, and to this extent he supports Eunapius' claim that the Goths used Christian bishops to deceive the emperors.[148] Nevertheless, he fails to mention that the Goths included among their number a large 'tribe' of monks. This is not to deny that there were monks among the Goths before they crossed into Roman territory. I merely note that Eunapius' account of their number and importance contrasts with Ammianus' failure to mention them. It is also difficult to believe that so many should have survived the persecution of Christians within Gothic territory during the 370s, even if they had enjoyed the protection of Fritigern, ruler of the Greuthungi, one of the larger Gothic groups.[149]

---

[146] Epiphanius, *Pan.* 70.14.5-6.
[147] Ambrose, *Ep.* 1.10.9.
[148] Amm. 31.12.8-9, 15.6.
[149] See P. Heather and J. Matthews, *The Goths in the Fourth Century* (Liverpool, 1991), pp. 103-31.

I argue that Eunapius compounded his initial mistake by claiming that the alleged Gothic monks had not been real monks in the Roman style primarily because it seems most unlikely that his original source would have claimed that a single tribe, 'Blackcloaks' or not, had all disguised themselves as monks. At best, Eunapius' source said only that the Goths had disguised some of their number as false bishops, and when Eunapius thought that he had read a reference to the presence of monks among the Goths, he then extended the anecdote concerning Gothic cunning to include their disguising themselves as monks as well as bishops.

This brings us back to Alaric in 396. While it remains possible that some Gothic monks may have crossed the Danube with their fellow Goths in 376, since the whole population was in flight, it is far more difficult to explain what the alleged monks were doing at Thermopylae in 396. In this case, the military context lends extra force to the argument that Eunapius has misinterpreted his source, that the 'Blackcloaks' at Thermopylae were not monks, but fellow barbarians from across the Danube, if not actually Goths also, and that this was why they assisted Alaric. They were barbarian soldiers in Roman service who defected to the enemy, with the result that their commander Gerontius was no longer able to hold the pass at Thermopylae. Contrary to Zosimus, therefore, Alaric did not send word of his approach to Gerontius as such, but to some of his forces under Gerontius whose defection left Gerontius himself with no choice but to retreat. This is not surprising, since barbarian elements within his army had already attempted to defect from Theodosius I to the usurper Magnus Maximus sometime during the 380s, although their exact military status remains a matter of controversy.[150] There is an obvious comparison here also with events in Phrygia in 399, when the *comes* Tribigild began his revolt with the support of Goths serving in the regular Roman forces, Greuthungi for the most part.[151] In short, the Gothic elements within the regular Roman forces had not been fully reconciled to their fate by 396, and this was why the 'Blackcloaks' defected to Alaric. Indeed, if the Gerontius who commanded the pass of Thermopylae in 396 is identifiable as the Gerontius who had massacred some Gothic troops at Tomi in the 380s,[152] as

---

[150] See Heather (n. 133), pp. 183-84 on Zosimus, *HN* 4.45.3.
[151] See A. Cameron and J. Long, *Barbarians and Politics at the Court of Arcadius* (Berkeley, 1993), pp. 111-16.
[152] Zosimus, *HN* 4.40.

some believe possible,[153] then one suspects that his attitude towards them may have been one of the factors which impelled the 'Blackcloaks' towards Alaric.

To conclude, therefore, Eunapius of Sardis has left a false impression of the strength of monasticism among the Goths during the last quarter of the 4th-century because of his misinterpretation of the name of a tribe called the 'Blackcloaks' in reference to monks, or the 'men-in-black' as he disparagingly called them. Arguments concerning the date of the conversion of the Goths to Christianity, or the degree of their Christianization, need to be revised accordingly.

---

[153] E.g. *PLRE I*, p. 394; Burns (n. 136), p. 157.